Business Logistics
Theoretical and Practical Perspectives with Analyses

TURKAY YILDIZ

Copyright © 2014 Turkay Yildiz

All rights reserved.

ISBN-13: 978-1-312-36311-3

DEDICATION

To my parents...

Table of Contents

PREFACE 7

PART I LOGISTICS SERVICES IN DEVELOPED AND DEVELOPING COUNTRIES 8

CHAPTER 1. A GLOBAL ANALYSIS OF LOGISTICS AND BUSINESS SERVICES IN DEVELOPED AND DEVELOPING COUNTRIES 9

    1. INTRODUCTION 10
    2. LITERATURE REVIEW 12
    3. DATA AND METHODS 18
        3.1 Two-Sample Comparison Statistics *19*
        3.2 Cluster analysis *26*
    4. FINDINGS AND DISCUSSION 27
    5. CONCLUSION 29
    6. REFERENCES 31
    APPENDIX 36

CHAPTER 2. THE PERFORMANCES OF LOGISTICS SERVICES IN DEVELOPED AND DEVELOPING COUNTRIES: A REVIEW AND CLUSTER ANALYSIS 43

    1. INTRODUCTION 44
    2. LITERATURE REVIEW 46
    3. DATA AND METHODS 49
        3.1 Correlations and regression analysis *51*
        3.2 Clustering *58*
    4. FINDINGS AND DISCUSSION 60
    5. CONCLUSION 67
    6. REFERENCES 69

PART II GLOBAL COMPETITIVENESS & LOGISTICS PERFORMANCE 74

CHAPTER 3. AN EMPIRICAL STUDY ON THE COMPLEX RELATIONSHIPS BETWEEN LOGISTICS PERFORMANCES AND GLOBAL COMPETITIVENESS 75

    1. INTRODUCTION 76
    2. LITERATURE REVIEW 77
    3. DATA AND METHODS 81
        3.1 Canonical correlation analysis of LPI and GCI scores *83*
        3.2 Structural equation modeling *87*

4. RESEARCH FINDINGS AND DISCUSSIONS 91
5. CONCLUSION 93
6. REFERENCES 95
APPENDIX 99
   Factor analysis of LPI *101*
   Factor analysis of GCI *102*
   SEM results for Pillars 1-9: *104*
   SEM results for Pillars 11-12: *106*

PART III LOGISTICS PERFORMANCE AND EDUCATION 108

CHAPTER 4. THE COMPLEX DYNAMICS OF THE RELATIONSHIP BETWEEN LOGISTICS PERFORMANCE AND EDUCATION 109

1. INTRODUCTION 110
2. LITERATURE REVIEW 111
3. DATA AND METHODS 113
   3.1 Canonical correlation analysis of logistics performance indicators and PISA scores *115*
   3.2 Ridge regression for logistics performance indicators versus raw PISA scores *118*
   3.3 Canonical correlation analysis of logistics performance indicators and GCI5 scores *120*
   3.4 Canonical correlation analysis of logistics performance indicators and IMD scores *122*
4. FINDINGS AND DISCUSSION 124
5. CONCLUSION 129
6. REFERENCES 129
APPENDIX 133
   Factor analysis of LPI and PISA scores *133*
   The test of the existence of linear relationships for LPI and PISA, LPI and GCI's 5th pillar, LPI and IMD's pillar *135*
   Factor analysis of LPI and IMD's scores *136*

PART IV TRANSPORT MODE & FUEL TYPE 141

CHAPTER 5. THE DYNAMIC RELATIONSHIPS BETWEEN THE CHOICES OF TRANSPORT MODE AND FUEL TYPE: THE CASE OF TURKEY 142

1. INTRODUCTION 143
2. LITERATURE REVIEW 145
3. DATA AND METHOD 148
   3.1 Data *148*

- 3.2 Method 150
  - 3.2.1 Unit root tests 150
  - 3.2.2 Co-integration test 156
  - 3.2.3 Causality test 156
- 4. FINDINGS AND DISCUSSION 158
- 5. CONCLUSION 161
- 6. REFERENCES 163
- APPENDIX 169

ABOUT THE AUTHOR 178

PREFACE

This book is the collection of my own studies in logistics, targeted to a broad readership. Although it is not intended for beginners in logistics, they might find the whole book interesting and beneficial.

The book consists of 4 parts and 5 chapters. The first part deals with the logistics services in developed and developing countries, while the second part covers global competitiveness and logistics performance. The third part is about the relationship between the logistics performance and education and, finally, the fourth part examines the relationship between the choices of transport mode and fuel type.

All the chapters in this book are independent of each other, with each one reflecting my own experience, analyses and results. I hope you will find this book useful, informative and appropriate for your needs.

Turkay Yildiz, M.A., Ph.D.
Izmir, Turkey
2014

Part I
Logistics Services in Developed and Developing Countries

Chapter 1. A global analysis of logistics and business services in developed and developing countries

Abstract. Developed countries have well-developed infrastructure, expertise, and enough capital to finance and thus provide the best logistics services, while developing countries are faced with many challenges to fully exploit the opportunities offered in the global economy. The logistics services and transportation infrastructure that exists in many developing countries is poorly maintained and managed and thereby insufficient to support advanced logistics activities. Although the governments of these countries are aware of these infrastructural shortcomings, they usually have insufficient capital and expertise to make improvements. This study explores the statistically significant differences in logistics performance over the past five years based on the World Bank's Doing Business indicators and by analyzing various income groups for developed and developing countries. The results indicate that significant differences in logistics performance among developed countries have existed over the past five years. Moreover, across all income levels, significant differences exist mainly in export-related indicators and other business indicators in the Doing Business data.

Keywords: logistics performance, doing business, developed and developing, progress in performance, income groups, policy

1. Introduction

In our fast-paced, multi-polar global economy, some developing countries have become economic powers, while others are rapidly becoming additional sources of growth (World Bank 2011a). These countries tend to provide the demand that drives the global economy (World Bank 2011a).

As important importers of capital goods and services, developing countries have accounted for more than half the growth in global demand for imports since 2000 (World Bank 2011a). Millions of people in transition and developing countries are entering the world economy, as their incomes and standards of living increase (World Bank 2011a). However, developing countries face many challenges, including the traditional trade barriers (tariff and non-tariff barriers) that impede access to the market (McLinden *et al.* 2010). Although such barriers continue to restrict those products that provide developing countries with a comparative advantage such as agricultural goods, the average tariff level has dropped significantly in recent decades. Moreover, many of the poorest countries now have duty-free access to high-income markets (McLinden *et al.* 2010).

Developing countries are increasingly concerned about the uneven pattern of growth they are experiencing (Brar *et al.* 2010). Different leading and lagging indicators are becoming more pronounced and governments are seeking to explore various initiatives to generate internal growth (Brar *et al.* 2010). This is especially true for large middle-income countries, which also happens to be where a large proportion of the world's poorest people reside (Brar *et al.* 2010).

Developing countries, however, also face new and complex challenges (World Bank 2011b). The destructive global financial crisis of 2007/08 interrupted their economic growth and slowed the pace of poverty reduction, while the recovery remains uncertain and uneven. Moreover, a pandemic is threatening the lives of millions, food security is undermining the well-being of many in conflict-affected regions, and the need to mitigate the effects of climate change, especially in developing countries, is more relevant than ever before (World Bank 2011b).

Effective logistics performance plays a key role in the global flow of goods and services and in the ability of countries to attract and sustain investment (Hausman *et al.* 2013). The inefficiency of logistics has been identified as a major constraint to productivity and competitiveness in developing countries by previous studies of investment and trade facilitation conditions (so-called "behind the border" issues) (Hausman *et al.* 2013). In the face of the challenges of global competition, businesses are becoming more focused on customer needs and finding ways in which to reduce costs, improve quality and meet the growing expectations of their customers (Lai and Cheng 2009). For this purpose, many of them have found logistics to be an area in which to reduce costs and improve the benefits of services (Lai and Cheng 2009).

The transport infrastructure that exists in many developing countries is often poorly maintained and managed and thus insufficient to support advanced logistics activities. Although the governments of these countries are aware of these infrastructural shortcomings, they usually have insufficient capital and expertise to make improvements. Indeed, few significant improvements in logistics performance in developing countries have been witnessed over the past five years. Further, it remains uncertain according to which business indicators developed and developing economies have common significant differences.

This study explores the statistically significant differences in logistics performance over the past five years based on the World Bank's Doing Business indicators and by analyzing various income groups for developed and developing countries. The results indicate that significant differences in logistics performance among developed countries have existed over the past five years. Moreover, across all income levels, significant differences exist mainly in export-related indicators and other business indicators in the Doing Business data.

The remainder of this study is organized as follows. Section 2 reviews the literature on logistics and business services. Section 3 introduces the data and methods used for the presented analysis. Section 4 presents and discusses the empirical findings. The study is concluded in Section 5.

2. Literature review

Saez (2010) found that, according to some estimates, the logistics sector represents approximately 14 percent of global gross domestic product (GDP). In addition, logistics costs represent 10 to 17 percent of GDP in industrialized countries (Saez 2010). Moreover, the logistics sector has increased by approximately 10 percent per year since the early 1990s (Saez 2010), with the fastest growth rates being seen by 3PL logistics and fourth party services (companies that coordinate activities among 3PLs) followed by international container shipping and airfreight services (Saez 2010). In addition, research shows that improving logistics performance in low-income countries to the middle-income average could boost trade by 15 percent or more (Fardoust *et al.* 2010).

Haddad and Shepherd (2011) pointed out that the likely future drivers of export growth and diversification in developing countries will be developing countries themselves, as these states play a vital role through trade. GDP growth in developing countries with low and middle incomes has already resulted in an increase in import demand, which has played an important role in stimulating exports and promoting export diversification in low-income countries. For example, countries with low and middle incomes accounted for 31 percent of world imports in 2008 (Haddad and Shepherd 2011).

Dadush and Shaw (2011) found that even in the largest developing countries, national economies are being overshadowed by the size and sophistication of the global market. In recent years, developing countries have increased remarkably in importance both as importers and exporters, and in most cases, trade has been essential to their economic success (Dadush and Shaw 2011). Indeed, even though rapid export growth does not guarantee success, no country has sustained growth without increasing its quota of exports (Dadush and Shaw 2011). In this sense, while growth conditions must be put in place at home, increases in exports and imports are often where development succeeds or fails on the world stage (Dadush and Shaw 2011).

Shamim (2009) pointed out that the supply chain (also logistics network or supply network) is a coordinated system of organizations, people, activities, information, and resources involved in moving a product or service in a physical or virtual manner from a supplier to a customer. Supply chain activities (also value chain or life cycle processes) transform raw materials and components into a finished product that is delivered to the end user (Shamim 2009). Supply chains link value chains (Shamim 2009). Logistics, which consists of (i) transportation (inbound/outbound), (ii) warehousing, (iii) inventory, (iv) materials management, (v) unitization, and (vi) communications, helps maintain demand through marketing efforts (Muthiah 2010).

Saez (2010) stated that logistics services are traditionally managed within firms. More recently, however, such services have been transferred to specialized companies, known as third-party logistics or 3PL providers, which offer integrated transportation, warehousing, inventory management, order processing, customs brokerage, and other logistics services (Saez 2010). The most commonly outsourced activities of domestic and international freight are warehousing, customs clearance and brokerage, and forwarding (Saez 2010). 3PL firms provide logistics services to meet the specific needs and specifications of its customers (Saez 2010). Although outsourcing has been particularly intense in industrialized countries, companies in developing countries are also now beginning to outsource logistics services (Saez 2010).

Muthiah (2010) highlighted that the overall effect of this change is that the goal of logistics is becoming to achieve a target level of customer service at the lowest possible total cost. That is, it aims to service the demand created by marketing efforts (Muthiah 2010). By meeting effective service demand, customer satisfaction is achieved and a network of satisfied customers is built, which leads to increases in market share and competitive advantage and thus increased profitability (Muthiah 2010). It was further noted by Saez (2010) that according to some estimates, the logistics industry accounts for about 14 percent of global GDP. In addition, logistics costs can be about 10 to 17 percent of GDP in industrialized countries (Saez 2010). Moreover, the logistics industry has grown by about 10 percent per year since the early 1990s (Saez 2010).

Justin and Pleskovic (2009) stated that technological advances in IT and logistics systems, which lead to lower transport and communication costs and a subsequent reduction in tariffs and other barriers to trade, have changed the economic landscapes of countries, industries, and individual firms. Multinational corporations have been the key agents in this transformation by creating global production and marketing networks that actively interact with each other (Justin and Pleskovic 2009). Further, according to Saez (2010), the highest rates of growth are shown by 3PL and 4PL providers (the latter being companies that coordinate activities among 3PLs) as well as international container shipping and airfreight firms. Fardoust *et al.* (2010) also indicated that economic growth in developing countries is increasingly important for global growth. Owing to fast-growing emerging markets, developing countries now make up about half of global growth (Fardoust *et al.* 2010).

As noted by McLinden *et al.* (2010), trade and transport facilitation reform has become a key priority for development in recent years. Several factors contribute to the growing importance of this program for policymakers and development agencies (McLinden *et al.* 2010). Fardoust *et al.* (2010) stated that for less developed countries, building trade capacity is as important as improving access to markets in the promotion of trade. Thus, a further priority is to strengthen support for trade facilitation in terms of border barriers to trade improvements, trade-related infrastructure, regulations, and logistics activities such as customs and standards compliance (Fardoust *et al.* 2010). McLinden *et al.* (2010) indicated that the economic benefits of trade are now widely recognized, especially given that logistics costs often have a greater impact on trade than tariffs do. Recent empirical findings have also provided evidence on the price of inefficiency and the potential large income from investments that can be obtained through targeted reforms (McLinden *et al.* 2010).

As acknowledged by McLinden *et al.* (2010), countries need to reduce trading costs and enhance export competitiveness, trade, and supportive policies in order to remain competitive. While all these factors are important, the reform of trade facilitation should be emphasized, as it plays an important role in improving national competitiveness (McLinden *et al.* 2010). McLinden *et al.* (2010) also emphasized that countries with better logistics services can grow faster, become more competitive, and increase their trade investments. Indeed, studies show that increasing the efficiency of logistics in low-income countries to the middle-income average could increase trade by about 15 percent, which would benefit all firms and consumers through lower prices and better services (McLinden et al. 2010). These authors also acknowledged that a key factor in determining the competitiveness of exporters from developing countries is the national investment climate and business environment, which are the main determinants of costs and thus profitability.

The assembled evidence further highlights the large gap in performance between low- and high-income countries as well as the significant differences between countries with similar levels of development (McLinden et al. 2010). Fardoust et al. (2010) emphasized that trade logistics in developing countries should be further supported. In this regard, reducing trade costs by improving trade rules, trade logistics, and infrastructure would make a valuable contribution to economic development (Fardoust et al. 2010). In addition, more assistance should be directed towards low-income countries, which currently receive only half of total aid (Fardoust et al. 2010). Wood et al. (2002) added that logistics systems and business practices differ around the world owing to cultural differences, which need to be overcome for effective business communication and transactions to occur.

Saez (2010) found that progress in the fields of transport and ICT has enabled production fragmentation and that logistics services are an important infrastructure for developing trade in these tasks. Cross-border communication between tasks requires an efficient logistics services sector for the production of goods, while the quality of the logistics infrastructure can influence firm decisions about the countries in which to open space, vendors to rely on, and how to enter consumer markets (Saez 2010). In addition, it has been argued by Hesse (2008) that recent innovations in technology and management have actually led to significant changes in logistics operations. This is especially true for integrated upstream supply chain management and the reorganization of distribution networks to have a much higher spatial coverage than before (Hesse 2008). Owing to these changes, logistics has changed radically in the post-war period, primarily because of demand for services by production and retail firms, but also into a powerful system that lays the foundation for a flexible, highly redistributive economy (Hesse 2008). These changes are likely to affect the respective parts of the production or retail process rather than being determined by the place and time of production or distribution (Hesse 2008).

Studies of logistics, business and transportation in relation to performance have been performed by many authors. This research stream reflects the increasing amount of international literature in this field based on various perspectives. For example, the factors that explain country-level logistics performances were analyzed by Gogoneata (2008), while trade policy, trade costs and developing country trade were examined by Hoekman and Nicita (2011). In addition, the impact of trade logistics performance on trade was investigated by Hausman *et al.* (2013).

In the same vein, logistics performance in the context of the supply chain was investigated by Green *et al.* (2008), while Liu *et al.* (2011) explored 3PL performance and service delivery. The relation between performance and logistics service delivery was assessed by Liu and Lyons (2011), the integration of supply chain relationships between product/process strategy and performance services was studied by Droge *et al.* (2012), the efficiency, effectiveness and differentiation of logistics performance was the focus of Fugate *et al.* (2010) and Grawe *et al.* (2011) synthesized knowledge and innovative logistics processes in order to increase operational flexibility and performance.

A comparative analysis of logistics performance and customer satisfaction among primary and secondary suppliers was carried out by Leuschner *et al.* (2012), while the degree to which prioritization issues affect the performance of logistics was assessed by Ruamsook *et al.* (2009). Other authors have examined user influence on the relationship between forecast accuracy, demand and logistics performance (Smith and Mentzer 2010) and logistics sophistication, manufacturing segments and the choice of logistics providers (Wanke *et al.* 2007).

The study of digitizing logistics and its impact on performance was conducted by Lai *et al.* (2010). Earlier, Lai *et al.* (2008) theoretically investigated the impact of electronic integration on logistics performance, while an analysis of the moderating roles of risks and the effectiveness of the logistics performance–customer loyalty nexus in electronic commerce was performed by Ramanathan (2010).

In terms of the regional breakdown of previous studies, logistics capacity and the performance of large manufacturing companies in Taiwan was investigated by Shang and Marlow (2005), the lead-times of food retailers in the UK and Greek markets were explored by Menachof *et al.* (2009), how logistical resources influence the performance of logistics providers in Malaysia was the focus of Karia and Wong (2013) and the work environment, commitment of resources and reverse logistics performance in the Taiwanese high-tech sector was researched by Huang *et al.* (2012).

Methodologically, multiple evaluation criteria and fuzzy-based logistics performance for intermodal transport were examined by Hanaoka and Kunadhamraks (2009), while Colledani and Tolio (2011) proposed an integrated analysis of the quality of production logistics, while reverse logistics and superior performance through IT commitments were analyzed by Daugherty *et al.* (2005).

On a sectoral basis, Garcia *et al.* (2012) developed a framework for measuring the performance of logistics in the wine industry, while a similar study in the automotive industry was conducted by Schmitz and Platts (2004). Further, another study assessed the distribution of pharmaceutical products and examined how to combine business performance and logistics individually (Spindler 2010).

The impact of timely information on organizational performance in a supply chain was investigated by Green *et al.* (2007), while Hamdan and Rogers (2008) and Kayakutlu and Buyukozkan (2011) evaluated the efficiency of 3PL logistics operations. Other authors provided a dynamic assessment of the performance of supply chains in emerging markets (Cedillo-Campos and Sanchez-Ramirez 2013) and explored how to improve the performance of 3PL providers by using an integrated approach with a logistics information system (Liu *et al.* 2008).

Based on the foregoing, the present study adds another dimension to the existing literature. In this regard, by using statistical methods, this study contributes to a better understanding for policymakers. Specifically, it differs from previous works in that it investigates statistically significant relationships for logistics performance among the various income levels of developing and developed countries.

3. Data and methods

Data were derived from a survey of logistics efficiency by the World Bank in partnership with academic and international institutions and private companies and individuals engaged in international logistics efficiency. This index, which is used in this analysis evaluates the effectiveness of logistics in six aspects (see definitions below), based on more than 5000 country assessments by nearly 1000 international freight forwarders World Bank (2011b). Respondents evaluated eight markets on these six core dimensions on a five-point scale from 1 (worst) to 5 (best). The markets were randomly chosen based on the most important export and import markets of the respondent's country and those of neighboring countries that connect them with international markets World Bank (2011b). The results for these six areas were then averaged over all respondents and merged into a single measure (World Bank 2011c). The resulting logistics performance index (LPI) reflects the perception of the country's logistics sector based on the (i) efficiency of customs clearance processes (CUST), (ii) quality of trade and transport-related infrastructure (INFR), (iii) ease of organizing supplies at competitive prices (ITRN), (iv) quality of logistics services (LOGS), (v) ability to track the movement of goods (TRAC), and (vi) frequency of deliveries within the scheduled time (TIME) (World Bank 2011c). The LPI thus helps identify areas where improvements are most needed (Handjiski and Sestovic 2011).

The Doing Business project, the annual World Bank publication launched in 2004, aims to promote private-sector development in four ways: to motivate benchmarking through the reform of the country, to develop reforms to enrich international initiatives on development effectiveness, and to inform theory (World Bank 2008). The Doing Business project takes a different approach from perception surveys. It focuses on domestic, primarily small and medium-sized companies and uses measurements applicable to their life cycles. Based on standardized case studies, it thus provides quantitative indicators of business regulation that can be compared across 183 countries and over time. This approach is complementary to the study of perception in terms of the major obstacles to business, as experienced by the enterprises themselves, set out in the regulations that apply to them (World Bank 2012).

3.1 Two-Sample Comparison Statistics

This procedure compares two samples of data. It calculates various statistics for each sample and runs several tests to determine whether there are any statistically significant differences between them. Table A1(a, b) in the appendix presents the summary statistics for the two samples of data in this study. Of particular interest are the standardized skewness and standardized kurtosis tests, which are used to determine whether the samples are normally distributed. The standardized skewness test looks for the non-existence of symmetry in the data, whereas the standardized kurtosis test focuses on distributional shape, which is either flat or peaked compared with the normal distribution. The values of these statistical data outside the range of -2 to +2 show significant departures from normality, which would tend to invalidate the tests, which compare standard deviations. In this case, some variables seem to have standardized skewness values outside the normal range. Therefore, a test to compare medians and therefore ascertain statistical significance is appropriate. In this regard, the Mann–Whitney W-test is performed to compare the medians of the two samples. This test is constructed by combining the two samples, sorting the data from smallest to largest, and comparing the average ranks of the two samples in the combined data. Statistically significant p values are marked by * in Table 1.

Table 1. Comparison of medians.

Economies	Statistics	CUST	INFR	ITRN	LOGS	TRAC	TIME	OVRL
World	Av. rank 2012	161.41	167.33	161.78	161.19	163.04	158.76	164.17
	Av. rank 2007	141.31	135.25	140.95	141.55	139.65	144.04	138.49
	W	9881.50	8977.00	9826.00	9915.50	9632.50	10287.5	9460.00
	P	0.02**	0.00***	0.02**	0.03**	0.01**	0.07*	0.01**
Emerging and Developing	Av. rank 2012	131.40	137.64	132.35	131.12	132.92	129.29	134.76
	Av. rank 2007	106.28	99.88	105.30	106.57	104.72	108.44	102.83
	W	5531.50	4783.50	5417.50	5566.00	5349.50	5785.00	5128.50
	P	0.00***	0.00***	0.00***	0.00***	0.00***	0.01**	0.00***
Major Advanced Economies (G7)	Av. rank 2012	7.14	8.00	5.50	7.29	7.00	7.57	7.43
	Av. rank 2007	7.86	7.00	9.50	7.71	8.00	7.43	7.57
	W	27.00	21.00	38.50	26.00	28.00	24.00	25.00
	P	0.60	0.35	0.96	0.55	0.65	0.50	0.50
European Union	Av. rank 2012	26.40	27.10	25.71	26.54	26.56	24.92	26.27
	Av. rank 2007	25.58	24.86	26.30	25.44	25.42	27.12	25.72
	W	314.50	296.50	332.50	311.00	310.50	353.00	318.00
	P	0.43	0.30	0.55	0.40	0.40	0.70	0.45
Middle East and North Africa	Av. rank 2012	20.08	20.90	21.03	19.95	20.20	19.88	20.63
	Av. rank 2007	18.86	17.94	17.81	19.00	18.72	19.08	18.25
	W	168.50	152.00	149.50	171.00	166.00	172.50	157.50
	P	0.37	0.21	0.19	0.40	0.35	0.42	0.26
Sub Saharan Africa	Av. rank 2012	38.16	42.10	40.57	40.20	40.26	38.97	41.41
	Av. rank 2007	33.90	30.07	31.56	31.92	31.86	33.11	30.74
	W	554.50	416.50	470.00	483.00	481.00	526.00	440.50
	P	0.19	0.01**	0.03**	0.05*	0.04**	0.12	0.01**
Latin America and Caribbean	Av. rank 2012	24.57	25.36	25.00	24.60	24.43	23.98	24.90
	Av. rank 2007	18.43	17.64	18.00	18.40	18.57	19.02	18.10
	W	156.00	139.50	147.00	155.50	159.00	168.50	149.00
	P	0.05*	0.02**	0.03**	0.05*	0.06*	0.10	0.04**
Developing Asia	Av. rank 2012	20.47	20.94	19.78	20.08	20.69	19.67	20.75
	Av. rank 2007	16.53	16.06	17.22	16.92	16.31	17.33	16.25
	W	126.50	118.00	139.00	133.50	122.50	141.00	121.50
	P	0.13	0.08*	0.24	0.19	0.11	0.26	0.10
Euro Area	Av. rank 2012	16.91	17.29	17.41	16.94	17.38	15.15	16.68
	Av. rank 2007	17.09	16.69	16.56	17.06	16.59	18.97	17.34
	W	137.50	131.00	129.00	137.00	129.50	167.50	141.50
	P	0.51	0.44	0.41	0.51	0.41	0.87	0.57
Central and Eastern Europe	Av. rank 2012	15.08	15.88	13.88	14.35	15.46	14.96	15.27
	Av. rank 2007	10.75	9.88	12.04	11.54	10.33	10.88	10.54
	W	51.00	40.50	66.50	60.50	46.00	52.50	48.50
	P	0.07*	0.02**	0.27	0.18	0.04**	0.09*	0.06*
Advanced Economies	Av. rank 2012	31.80	32.95	29.98	31.41	31.23	28.61	31.14
	Av. rank 2007	32.21	31.02	34.08	32.61	32.79	35.50	32.89
	W	502.50	465.50	560.50	515.00	520.50	604.50	523.50
	P	0.53	0.34	0.81	0.60	0.63	0.93	0.64
Commonwealth of Independent States	Av. rank 2012	13.73	14.91	13.55	14.23	14.14	12.77	14.41
	Av. rank 2007	8.00	6.70	8.20	7.45	7.55	9.05	7.25
	W	25.00	12.00	27.00	19.50	20.50	35.50	17.50
	P	0.02**	0.00***	0.03**	0.01**	0.01**	0.09*	0.00***
ASEAN – 5	Av. rank 2012	4.60	5.80	5.60	5.80	5.10	6.00	6.00
	Av. rank 2007	6.40	5.20	5.40	5.20	5.90	5.00	5.00
	W	17.00	11.00	12.00	11.00	10.50	10.00	10.00
	P	0.80	0.42	0.50	0.42	0.38	0.34	0.34
Other Advanced Economies	Av. rank 2012	11.82	12.05	9.95	10.91	11.18	9.95	10.86
	Av. rank 2007	11.18	10.95	13.05	12.09	11.82	13.05	12.14
	W	57.00	54.50	77.50	67.00	64.00	77.50	67.50
	P	0.42	0.36	0.86	0.65	0.58	0.86	0.67

Null hypothesis : median (2012) = median (2007)
Alt. Hypothesis : median (2012) > median (2007)
*** denotes statistically significant at 1% level, ** denotes statistically significant at 5% level
* denotes statistically significant at 10% level

The World Bank's Doing Business project covers two types of data. The first type is derived from the testimony of the laws and regulations. The second type uses time and motion indicators in order to measure the efficiency and complexity of achieving a regulatory goal (e.g., granting the legal identity of a business) (World Bank 2011a). In this way, Doing Business provides the quantitative rules for domestic small and medium-sized enterprises in terms of starting a business, dealing with construction permits, getting electricity, registering property, getting credit, protecting investors, paying taxes, conducting international trade, enforcing contracts, and resolving insolvency. It also examines the position of hiring employees (World Bank 2012) (see Table 2).

Table 2. Doing Business indicators.

Main topics	Indicator code	Indicator Name
1. Starting a business (Reg)	Reg1	Cost to start a business (% of income per capita)
	Reg2	Minimum paid-in capital required to start a business (% of income per capita)
	Reg3	Procedures required to start a business (number)
	Reg4	Time required to start a business (days)
2. Dealing with construction permits (Dcp)	Dcp1	Cost to build a warehouse (% of income per capita)
	Dcp2	Procedures required to build a warehouse (number)
	Dcp3	Time required to build a warehouse (days)
3. Getting electricity (Ge)	Ge1	Cost to get electricity (% of income per capita)
	Ge2	Procedures required to connect to electricity (number)
	Ge3	Time required to connect to electricity (days)
4. Registering property (Rp)	Rp1	Cost to register property (% of property value)
	Rp2	Procedures required to register property (number)
	Rp3	Time required to register property (days)
5. Getting credit (Crd)	Crd1	Credit: Strength of legal rights index (0=weak to 10=strong)
	Crd2	Depth of credit information index (0=low to 6=high)
	Crd3	Private credit bureau coverage (% of adults)
	Crd4	Public credit registry coverage (% of adults)
6. Protecting investors (Pi)	Pi1	Ease of shareholder suits index (0 to 10)
	Pi2	Extent of director liability index (0 to 10)
	Pi3	Extent of disclosure index (0 to 10)
	Pi4	Strength of investor protection index (0 to 10)
7. Paying taxes (Tax)	Tax1	Tax payments (number)
	Tax2	Time to prepare and pay taxes (hours)
	Tax3	Total tax rate (% of profit)
	Tax4	Profit tax (%)
	Tax5	Labor tax and contributions (%)
	Tax6	Other taxes (%)
8. Trading across borders (Exp)	Exp1	Trade: Cost to export (US$ per container)
	Exp2	Trade: Cost to import (US$ per container)
	Exp3	Trade: Documents to export (number)
	Exp4	Trade: Documents to import (number)
	Exp5	Trade: Time to export (day)
	Exp6	Trade: Time to import (days)
9. Enforcing contracts (Ec)	Ec1	Cost to enforce a contract (% of claim)
	Ec2	Procedures required to enforce a contract (number)
	Ec3	Time required to enforce a contract (days)
10. Resolving insolvency (Isv)	Isv1	Resolving Insolvency: cost (% of estate)
	Isv2	Resolving Insolvency: recovery rate (cents on the dollar)
	Isv3	Time to resolve insolvency (years)

In the next step, the Shapiro–Wilk test is performed to test for the normality of the data. The failure of the test, marked by the (-) symbol, indicates that the data vary significantly from the pattern expected if they were drawn from a population with a normal distribution. On the other hand, (+) indicates that the data match the pattern expected if they were drawn from a population with a normal distribution (see Table 3). Most of the values of these statistics indicate significant departures from normality, which would tend to invalidate the tests. Countries are labeled high-income countries (HIC), upper middle-income countries (UMC), middle-income countries (MIC), lower middle-income countries (LMC), and low-income countries (LIC) (See for country classifications: http://data.worldbank.org/about/country-classifications).

Table 3. Shapiro–Wilk test for normality.

Indicators	HIC Stat.	p		UMC Stat.	p		MIC Stat.	p		LMC Stat.	p		LIC Stat.	p	
Reg1	0.386	< 0.001	-	0.548	< 0.001	-	0.717	< 0.001	-	0.805	< 0.001	-	0.876	0.001	-
Reg2	0.464	< 0.001	-	0.505	< 0.001	-	0.448	< 0.001	-	0.562	< 0.001	-	0.745	< 0.001	-
Reg3	0.91	0.001	-	0.91	0.001	-	0.951	< 0.001	-	0.97	0.211	+	0.947	0.11	+
Reg4	0.568	< 0.001	-	0.306	< 0.001	-	0.324	< 0.001	-	0.783	< 0.001	-	0.808	< 0.001	-
Dcp1	0.573	< 0.001	-	0.619	< 0.001	-	0.615	< 0.001	-	0.665	< 0.001	-	0.689	< 0.001	-
Dcp2	0.87	< 0.001	-	0.893	< 0.001	-	0.903	< 0.001	-	0.908	< 0.001	-	0.877	0.002	-
Dcp3	0.807	< 0.001	-	0.903	< 0.001	-	0.906	< 0.001	-	0.902	< 0.001	-	0.652	< 0.001	-
Ge1	0.791	< 0.001	-	0.879	< 0.001	-	0.662	< 0.001	-	0.744	< 0.001	-	0.759	< 0.001	-
Ge2	0.889	< 0.001	-	0.905	< 0.001	-	0.919	< 0.001	-	0.918	0.001	-	0.853	< 0.001	-
Ge3	0.863	< 0.001	-	0.921	0.003	-	0.898	< 0.001	-	0.866	< 0.001	-	0.731	< 0.001	-
Rp1	0.91	0.001	-	0.926	0.004	-	0.858	< 0.001	-	0.83	< 0.001	-	0.953	0.162	+
Rp2	0.966	0.17	+	0.934	0.009	-	0.919	< 0.001	-	0.891	< 0.001	-	0.927	0.029	-
Rp3	0.663	< 0.001	-	0.699	< 0.001	-	0.561	< 0.001	-	0.515	< 0.001	-	0.703	< 0.001	-
Crd1	0.921	0.003	-	0.949	0.034	-	0.95	< 0.001	-	0.92	0.002	-	0.895	0.004	-
Crd2	0.775	< 0.001	-	0.751	< 0.001	-	0.817	< 0.001	-	0.855	< 0.001	-	0.845	< 0.001	-
Crd3	0.808	< 0.001	-	0.798	< 0.001	-	0.728	< 0.001	-	0.652	< 0.001	-	0.387	< 0.001	-
Crd4	0.445	< 0.001	-	0.805	< 0.001	-	0.741	< 0.001	-	0.673	< 0.001	-	0.524	< 0.001	-
Pi1	0.938	0.012	-	0.953	0.051	+	0.94	< 0.001	-	0.907	< 0.001	-	0.948	0.114	+
Pi2	0.938	0.013	-	0.904	< 0.001	-	0.94	< 0.001	-	0.942	0.012	-	0.822	< 0.001	-
Pi3	0.951	0.039	-	0.961	0.101	+	0.97	0.02	-	0.961	0.083	+	0.918	0.016	-
Pi4	0.967	0.182	+	0.961	0.102	+	0.981	0.154	+	0.971	0.216	+	0.97	0.481	+
Tax1	0.848	< 0.001	-	0.874	< 0.001	-	0.957	0.002	-	0.971	0.213	+	0.978	0.734	+
Tax2	0.922	0.003	-	0.441	< 0.001	-	0.552	< 0.001	-	0.798	< 0.001	-	0.815	< 0.001	-
Tax3	0.974	0.361	+	0.912	0.001	-	0.925	< 0.001	-	0.914	0.001	-	0.543	< 0.001	-
Tax4	0.964	0.136	+	0.84	< 0.001	-	0.917	< 0.001	-	0.953	0.037	-	0.933	0.042	-
Tax5	0.891	< 0.001	-	0.956	0.063	+	0.955	0.002	-	0.961	0.085	+	0.941	0.073	+
Tax6	0.697	< 0.001	-	0.526	< 0.001	-	0.543	< 0.001	-	0.546	< 0.001	-	0.538	< 0.001	-
Exp1	0.972	0.296	+	0.831	< 0.001	-	0.824	< 0.001	-	0.812	< 0.001	-	0.804	< 0.001	-
Exp2	0.921	0.003	-	0.908	< 0.001	-	0.791	< 0.001	-	0.723	< 0.001	-	0.815	< 0.001	-
Exp3	0.934	0.009	-	0.917	0.002	-	0.934	< 0.001	-	0.939	0.009	-	0.946	0.1	+
Exp4	0.947	0.029	-	0.962	0.12	+	0.96	0.004	-	0.954	0.041	-	0.868	< 0.001	-
Exp5	0.889	< 0.001	-	0.652	< 0.001	-	0.722	< 0.001	-	0.734	< 0.001	-	0.889	0.003	-
Exp6	0.765	< 0.001	-	0.776	< 0.001	-	0.786	< 0.001	-	0.763	< 0.001	-	0.849	< 0.001	-
Ec1	0.974	0.339	+	0.974	0.353	+	0.632	< 0.001	-	0.647	< 0.001	-	0.875	0.001	-
Ec2	0.964	0.139	+	0.965	0.148	+	0.978	0.084	+	0.96	0.077	+	0.932	0.039	-
Ec3	0.82	< 0.001	-	0.849	< 0.001	-	0.896	< 0.001	-	0.906	< 0.001	-	0.802	< 0.001	-
Isv1	0.895	< 0.001	-	0.871	< 0.001	-	0.879	< 0.001	-	0.893	< 0.001	-	0.844	< 0.001	-
Isv2	0.922	0.004	-	0.976	0.456	+	0.976	0.084	+	0.972	0.341	+	0.957	0.263	+
Isv3	0.933	0.01	-	0.937	0.014	-	0.937	< 0.001	-	0.919	0.004	-	0.945	0.127	+

The Kruskal–Wallis test is then performed to compare the medians of the samples in order to determine any statistically significant differences among them (see Table 4). This process tests the null hypothesis that the medians within each of the two columns are the same. The data from all the columns are first combined and ranked from smallest to largest. The average rank is then computed for the data in each column.

Table 4. Comparison of the medians of the pairs of income levels across indicators (p values).

Main topics	Indicator	HIC-UMC	HIC-MIC	HIC-LMC	HIC-LIC	UMC-LMC	UMC-LIC	MIC-LIC	LMC-LIC	UMC-MIC	MIC-LMC
Starting a business (Reg)	Reg1	0.061	0.000	0.000	0.000	0.001	0.000	0.000	0.035	0.204	0.277
	Reg2	0.821	1.000	1.000	1.000	1.000	0.238	0.595	1.000	1.000	1.000
	Reg3	0.475	0.049	0.040	0.530	1.000	1.000	1.000	1.000	1.000	1.000
	Reg4	0.141	0.002	0.001	0.015	1.000	1.000	1.000	1.000	1.000	1.000
Dealing with construction permits (Dcp)	Dcp1	0.050	0.000	0.000	0.000	0.249	0.000	0.000	0.038	1.000	1.000
	Dcp2	0.256	0.060	0.114	1.000	1.000	1.000	1.000	1.000	1.000	1.000
	Dcp3	0.356	0.713	1.000	0.156	1.000	1.000	1.000	1.000	1.000	1.000
Getting electricity (Ge)	Ge1	0.000	0.000	0.000	0.000	0.000	0.000	0.000	0.000	0.094	0.137
	Ge2	0.049	0.022	0.120	1.000	1.000	1.000	1.000	1.000	1.000	1.000
	Ge3	0.968	0.718	1.000	0.005	1.000	0.462	0.186	0.264	1.000	1.000
Registering property (Rp)	Rp1	1.000	1.000	1.000	0.007	1.000	0.106	0.062	0.194	1.000	1.000
	Rp2	0.081	0.064	0.373	0.165	1.000	1.000	1.000	1.000	1.000	1.000
	Rp3	1.000	0.184	0.006	0.000	0.048	0.002	0.073	1.000	1.000	1.000
Getting credit (Crd)	Crd1	0.028	0.007	0.034	0.156	1.000	1.000	1.000	1.000	1.000	1.000
	Crd2	1.000	1.000	0.271	0.000	0.269	0.000	0.001	0.071	1.000	1.000
	Crd3	0.063	0.000	0.000	0.000	0.460	0.004	0.028	0.660	1.000	1.000
	Crd4	0.025	0.116	1.000	1.000	0.943	0.163	0.658	1.000	1.000	1.000
Protecting investors (Pi)	Pi1	0.990	0.223	0.213	0.003	1.000	0.300	0.339	0.991	1.000	1.000
	Pi2	1.000	1.000	0.137	0.015	0.146	0.016	0.214	1.000	1.000	1.000
	Pi3	1.000	0.271	0.025	0.680	0.237	1.000	1.000	1.000	1.000	1.000
	Pi4	1.000	0.071	0.002	0.001	0.036	0.011	0.291	1.000	0.845	1.000
Paying taxes (Tax)	Tax1	0.074	0.000	0.000	0.000	0.000	0.000	0.015	1.000	0.154	0.215
	Tax2	0.000	0.000	0.000	0.000	1.000	1.000	1.000	1.000	1.000	1.000
	Tax3	1.000	1.000	1.000	0.088	1.000	0.687	0.084	0.041	1.000	1.000
	Tax4	1.000	1.000	1.000	0.698	1.000	1.000	1.000	1.000	1.000	1.000
	Tax5	1.000	0.925	0.353	0.256	1.000	1.000	1.000	1.000	1.000	1.000
	Tax6	0.315	1.000	1.000	0.000	0.950	0.042	0.000	0.000	1.000	1.000
Trading across borders (Exp)	Exp1	0.009	0.005	0.054	0.000	1.000	0.059	0.007	0.009	1.000	1.000
	Exp2	0.004	0.002	0.042	0.000	1.000	0.023	0.001	0.002	1.000	1.000
	Exp3	0.000	0.000	0.000	0.000	0.328	0.003	0.026	0.710	1.000	1.000
	Exp4	0.002	0.000	0.000	0.000	0.935	0.000	0.000	0.016	1.000	1.000
	Exp5	0.003	0.000	0.000	0.000	0.011	0.000	0.000	0.011	0.531	0.665
	Exp6	0.000	0.000	0.000	0.000	0.035	0.000	0.000	0.016	0.833	1.000
Enforcing contracts (Ec)	Ec1	0.008	0.000	0.000	0.000	0.981	0.000	0.001	0.062	1.000	1.000
	Ec2	0.897	0.026	0.005	0.012	0.788	0.851	1.000	1.000	1.000	1.000
	Ec3	1.000	0.586	0.661	1.000	1.000	1.000	1.000	1.000	1.000	1.000
Resolving insolvency (Isv)	Isv1	0.046	0.000	0.000	0.000	1.000	0.065	0.187	1.000	1.000	1.000
	Isv2	0.000	0.000	0.000	0.000	0.173	0.000	0.000	0.088	1.000	1.000
	Isv3	0.112	0.006	0.007	0.000	1.000	0.014	0.016	0.147	1.000	1.000

high-income countries (HIC), upper middle-income countries (UMC), middle-income countries (MIC), lower middle-income countries (LMC), low-income countries (LIC)

The highlighted cells in Table 4 indicate statistically significant differences, since the p value is less than 0.05; hence, there is a statistically significant difference among the medians at the 95% level.

3.2 Cluster analysis

Clustering is a widely used approach to segment a dataset into groups of related observations. It is used to understand the dataset and generate groups in a situation where the main objective is segmentation analysis. One of the most important components in any data clustering exercise is to estimate the distance between two observations (Myatt *et al.* 2009). Cluster analysis is the process of grouping observations based on similarity (visually as proximity), connectivity, and density. The result of the cluster analysis is called clustering (Anderson 2012). For the clustering of LPI scores, see Table 5.

Table 5. Summary of the clustering of the LPI (2012).

Indicator	Cluster number:	1	2	3	4	5	6	7	8	9
CUST	N	9	24	53	38	29	-	-	-	-
	(%)	5.88	15.69	34.64	24.84	18.95	-	-	-	-
	Mean	1.78	2.09	2.38	2.84	3.63	-	-	-	-
INFR	N	26	62	40	25	-	-	-	-	-
	(%)	16.99	40.52	26.14	16.34	-	-	-	-	-
	Mean	1.93	2.45	3.05	3.95	-	-	-	-	-
ITRN	N	1	13	30	42	36	31	-	-	-
	(%)	0.65	8.50	19.61	27.45	23.53	20.26	-	-	-
	Mean	1.57	1.97	2.39	2.69	3.02	3.59	-	-	-
LOGS	N	1	7	24	25	38	29	29	-	-
	(%)	0.65	4.58	15.69	16.34	24.84	18.95	18.95	-	-
	Mean	1.43	1.92	2.19	2.44	2.72	3.06	3.80	-	-
TRAC	N	6	13	31	40	32	31	-	-	-
	(%)	3.92	8.50	20.26	26.14	20.92	20.26	-	-	-
	Mean	1.76	2.10	2.40	2.69	3.16	3.83	-	-	-
TIME	N	1	6	10	21	25	27	36	27	-
	(%)	0.65	3.92	6.54	13.73	16.34	17.65	23.53	17.65	-
	Mean	1.67	2.29	2.53	2.74	2.93	3.19	3.58	4.11	-
OVRL	N	1	1	9	18	36	28	23	14	23
	(%)	0.65	0.65	5.88	11.76	23.53	18.30	15.03	9.15	15.03
	Mean	1.61	1.80	2.09	2.30	2.51	2.78	3.02	3.34	3.87

The cluster analysis procedure is designed to group observations or variables into clusters based upon their similarities. Cluster analysis is an exploratory tool designed to reveal natural groupings (or clusters) within the data. The raw data for the procedure can be in either of two forms: (1) n rows or cases, each containing the values of p quantitative variables, or (2) n rows and n columns if clustering observations or p rows and p columns if clustering variables, containing a measure of the 'distance' between all pairs of items (see Figure 1).

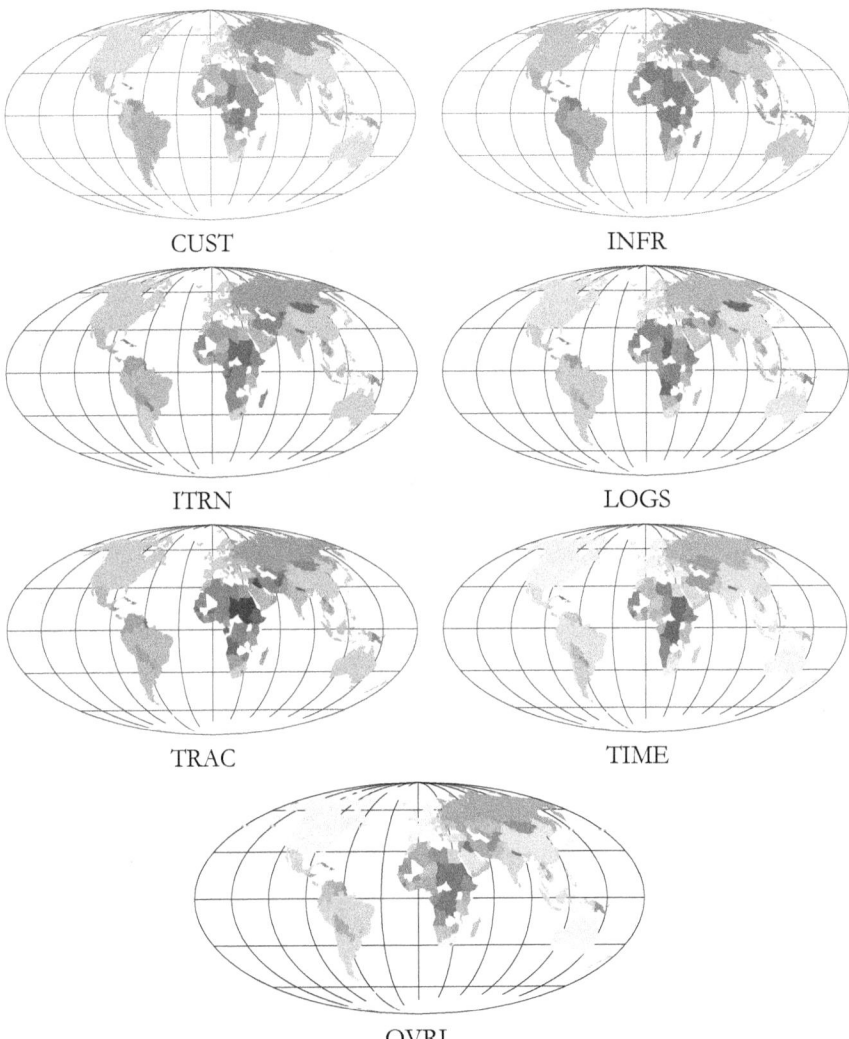

Figure 1. Logistics performances of countries (LPI 2012). In each figure, countries in lighter gray indicate high-performing countries, while countries in darker gray indicate low-performing countries. White regions mean unavailable data.

4. Findings and discussion

Based on the results presented in the previous section, the economies of some developing countries show significant improvements in logistics performances (see Table 1). Significant progress in all areas of logistics has been shown by emerging and developing economies, the Commonwealth of Independent States, and average economies. Sub-Saharan Africa has shown significant progress in all logistics performance areas except CUST and TIME. Central and Eastern Europe has shown significant progress in all logistics performance areas except ITRN and LOGS. The Latin America and Caribbean region has shown significant progress in all logistics performance areas except TIME. Developing Asia has only significant progress only in INFR. Economies in developed countries have not shown significant progress, as they have already achieved high LPI scores. The grouping of the sampled economies can be seen in Table A2 in the appendix.

Moreover, based on the comparison of the income levels of countries, the indicators of all trading across borders show significant differences (see Table 4). In addition, for the getting electricity (Ge1) indicator, there are significant differences among all income levels, as there are for the starting a business (Reg1) indicator, except between HIC and UMC. Meanwhile, dealing with construction permits (Dcp1) shows significant differences among all income levels, except between HIC and LMC. All other significant differences are highlighted in Table 4.

Table 5 shows the clustering results for all logistics performance indicators. Based on these results, countries can be grouped based on their similarities (Figure 1). For example, businesses in developed countries possess the best logistics and transportation specialists, systems, and infrastructure in the world (Wood *et al.* 2002). Managers take for granted such standards as advanced Internet technologies, high-capacity national highway systems, broadband fiber optic communications capabilities, seamless multi-modal transportation, modern port facilities, high-density air traffic control, and experienced professionals in logistics and specialist services (Wood *et al.* 2002).

However, what is perceived as the norm in developed countries is often an aspirational goal in many other places around the world (Wood *et al.* 2002). Developing countries are generally ranked low in the LPI, with the high cost of logistics in these countries serving as a major barrier to trade (Saez 2010). On average, logistics costs account for 18 percent of firm sales in

Latin America, reaching 32 percent in Chile, Argentina, Brazil, Paraguay, and Uruguay (World Bank 2006; Saez 2010). Further, the poor performance of Africa is mainly caused by the prevailing political and economic conditions, which prevent the development of modern logistics systems that promote trade and economic growth that are employed in industrialized countries (Gwilliam 2011). Hence, improving logistics services, as measured by the LPI, could provide the greatest benefits to African nations compared with any other components of the costs of trade (Saez 2010).

The emerging economies of the Third World (e.g., Sudan, Afghanistan, Haiti, and Ethiopia) are defined by low levels of industrialization, literacy, and per capita income (Wood *et al.* 2002). These economies focus on subsistence and maintenance, and they are often agrarian-based or have a large nomadic population (Wood *et al.* 2002). Moreover, the consumer markets are primitive, even in large cities, with the majority of consumption focused on meeting the necessities of life, such as food, clothing, and housing (Wood *et al.* 2002). First World nation-style consumer economies are almost completely unknown, or exist on a very small scale to meet the needs of elites (Wood *et al.* 2002). However, countries with abundant natural resources have new opportunities. To take advantage of these opportunities, the challenge for these economies is to improve the investment climate, create better institutions, and improve infrastructure, human capital, and knowledge while maintaining price stability (Haddad and Shepherd 2011).

5. Conclusion

Logistics performance was investigated in this study based on the World Bank's Doing Business indicators as well as various income groups for developed and developing countries. We showed that significant differences in logistics performance among developed countries have existed over the past five years. Across all income levels, significant differences were mainly found in exports and other related indicators in the Doing Business data.

Developed countries have well-developed infrastructure, expertise, and enough capital to finance and thereby provide the best logistics performance, whereas developing countries are faced with many challenges to fully exploit the opportunities offered in the global economy. The logistics services and transportation infrastructure that exists in many developing countries is poorly maintained and managed and thereby not sufficient to support advanced logistics activities. The governments of these countries might be aware of these infrastructural shortcomings; however, they usually have insufficient funds and expertise to make significant improvements.

6. References

Anderson, R. (2012). *Visual Data Mining: The VisMiner Approach (2nd Edition)*. Somerset, NJ, USA: Wiley, p 155.

Brar, S., Farley, S. E. Hawkins, R. (2010). *Logistics in Lagging Regions: Overcoming Local Barriers to Global Connectivity*. Herndon, VA, USA: World Bank Publications, 2010. p 1-7.

Cedillo-Campos, M., & Sanchez-Ramirez, C. (2013). Dynamic Self-Assessment of Supply Chains Performance: An Emerging Market Approach. *Journal of Applied Research and Technology*, 11, 338-347.

Colledani, M., & Tolio, T. (2011). Integrated analysis of quality and production logistics performance in manufacturing lines. *International Journal of Production Research*, 49(2), 485-518. doi: 10.1080/00207540903443246

Dadush, U., Shaw, W.J. (2011). *How Emerging Powers are Reshaping Globalization*. Washington, DC, USA: Carnegie Endowment for International Peace, p 6.

Daugherty, P. J., Richey, R. G., Genchev, S. E., Chen, H. Z. (2005). Reverse logistics: superior performance through focused resource commitments to information technology. *Transportation Research Part E-Logistics and Transportation Review*, 41(2), 77-92. doi: 10.1016/j.tre.2004.04.002

Droge, C., Vickery, S. K., & Jacobs, M. A. (2012). Does supply chain integration mediate the relationships between product/process strategy and service performance? An empirical study. *International Journal of Production Economics*, 137(2), 250-262. doi: 10.1016/j.ijpe.2012.02.005

Fardoust, S. (Editor), Kim, Y. (Editor), Sepulveda, C. P. (Editor). (2010). *Postcrisis Growth and Development: A Development Agenda for the G-20*. Herndon, VA, USA: World Bank Publications, p 148-265.

Fugate, B. S., Mentzer, J. T., & Stank, T. P. (2010). Logistics Performance: Efficiency, Effectiveness, and Differentiation. *Journal of Business Logistics*, 31(1), 43-+.

Garcia, F. A., Marchetta, M. G., Camargo, M., Morel, L., Forradellas, R. Q. (2012). A framework for measuring logistics performance in the wine industry. *International Journal of Production Economics*, 135(1), 284-298. doi: 10.1016/j.ijpe.2011.08.003

Gogoneata, B. (2008). An analysis of explanatory factors of logistics performance of a country. *Amfiteatru Economic*, 10(24), 143-156.

Grawe, S. J., Daugherty, P. J., & Roath, A. S. (2011). Knowledge Synthesis and Innovative Logistics Processes: Enhancing Operational Flexibility and Performance. *Journal of Business Logistics*, 32(1), 69-80.

Green, K. W., Whitten, D., & Inman, R. A. (2007). The impact of timely information on organisational performance in a supply chain. *Production Planning & Control*, 18(4), 274-282. doi: 10.1080/09537280701243926

Green, K. W., Whitten, D., & Inman, R. A. (2008). The impact of logistics performance on organizational performance in a supply chain context. *Supply Chain Management-An International Journal*, 13(4), 317-327. doi: 10.1108/13598540810882206

Gwilliam, K. M. (2011). *Africa's Transport Infrastructure: Mainstreaming Maintenance and Management*. Herndon, VA, USA: World Bank Publications, p 7.

Haddad, M. (Editor), Shepherd, B. (Editor). (2011). *Managing Openness: Trade and Outward-Oriented Growth after the Crisis*. Herndon, VA, USA: World Bank Publications, p 272-273.

Hamdan, A., & Rogers, K. J. (2008). Evaluating the efficiency of 3PL logistics operations. *International Journal of Production Economics*, 113(1), 235-244. doi: 10.1016/j.ijpe.2007.05.019

Hanaoka, S., & Kunadhamraks, P. (2009). Multiple Criteria and Fuzzy Based Evaluation of Logistics Performance for Intermodal Transportation. *Journal of Advanced Transportation*, 43(2), 123-153.

Handjiski, B., Sestovic, L. (2011). *World Bank Studies: Barriers to Trade in Services in the CEFTA Region*. Herndon, VA, USA: World Bank Publications, 2011. p 26.

Hausman, W. H., Lee, H. L., & Subramanian, U. (2013). The Impact of Logistics Performance on Trade. *Production and Operations Management*, 22(2), 236-252. doi: 10.1111/j.1937-5956.2011.01312.x

Hausman, W. H. (2004). Supply Chain Performance Metrics, *The Practice of Supply Chain Management: Where Theory and Application Converge*, 62, pp. 61-73: Springer US.

Hesse, M. (2008). *City as a Terminal: The Urban Context of Logistics and Freight Transport*. Abingdon, Oxon, GBR: Ashgate Publishing Group, p 19.

Hoekman, B., & Nicita, A. (2011). Trade Policy, Trade Costs, and Developing Country Trade. *World Development*, 39(12), 2069-2079. doi: 10.1016/j.worlddev.2011.05.013

Huang, Y. C., Wu, Y. C. J., & Rahman, S. (2012). The task environment, resource commitment and reverse logistics performance: Evidence from the Taiwanese high-tech sector. *Production Planning & Control*, 23(10-11), 851-863. doi: 10.1080/09537287.2011.642189

Justin, Y. L. (Editor), Pleskovic, B. (Editor). (2009). *Annual World Bank Conference on Development Economics (Global): Annual World Bank Conference on Development Economics 2009*, Global: People, Politics, and Globalization. Herndon, VA, USA: World Bank Publications, 2010. p 110.

Karia, N., & Wong, C. Y. (2013). The impact of logistics resources on the performance of Malaysian logistics service providers. *Production Planning & Control*, 24(7), 589-606. doi: 10.1080/09537287.2012.659871

Kayakutlu, G., & Buyukozkan, G. (2011). Assessing performance factors for a 3PL in a value chain. *International Journal of Production Economics*, 131(2), 441-452. doi: 10.1016/j.ijpe.2010.12.019

Krizman, A., & Ogorelc, A. (2010). Impact of Disturbing Factors On Cooperation In Logistics Outsourcing Performance: The Empirical Model. *Promet-Traffic & Transportation*, 22(3), 209-218.

Lai, K.-H., Cheng, T.C.E. (2009). *Just-in-Time Logistics*. Abingdon, Oxon, GBR: Ashgate Publishing Group, p 1.

Lai, K. H., Wong, C. W. Y., & Cheng, T. C. E. (2008). A coordination-theoretic investigation of the impact of electronic integration on logistics performance. *Information & Management*, 45(1), 10-20. doi: 10.1016/j.im.2007.05.007

Lai, K. H., Wong, C. W. Y., & Cheng, T. C. E. (2010). Bundling digitized logistics activities and its performance implications. *Industrial Marketing Management*, 39(2), 273-286. doi: 10.1016/j.indmarman.2008.08.002

Leuschner, R., Lambert, D. M., & Knemeyer, A. M. (2012). Logistics Performance, Customer Satisfaction, and Share of Business: A Comparison of Primary and Secondary Suppliers. *Journal of Business Logistics*, 33(3), 210-226. doi: 10.1111/j.2158-1592.2012.01053.x

Liu, C. L., & Lyons, A. C. (2011). An analysis of third-party logistics performance and service provision. *Transportation Research Part E-Logistics and Transportation Review*, 47(4), 547-570. doi: 10.1016/j.tre.2010.11.012

Liu, J. J., So, S. C. K., Choy, K. L., Lau, H., & Kwok, S. K. (2008). Performance improvement of third-party logistics providers - An integrated approach with a logistics information system. *International*

Journal of Technology Management, 42(3), 226-249. doi: 10.1504/ijtm.2008.018105

Liu, W. H., Xu, X. C., Ren, Z. X., & Peng, Y. (2011). An emergency order allocation model based on multi-provider in two-echelon logistics service supply chain. *Supply Chain Management-An International Journal*, 16(6), 391-400. doi: 10.1108/13598541111171101

McLinden, G. (Editor), Fanta, E. (Editor), Widdowson, D. (Editor). (2010). *Border Management Modernization*. Herndon, VA, USA: World Bank Publications, p iii-25.

Menachof, D. A., Bourlakis, M. A., & Makios, T. (2009). Order lead-time of grocery retailers in the UK and Greek markets. *Supply Chain Management-An International Journal*, 14(5), 349-358. doi: 10.1108/13598540910980260

Muthiah, K. V. (2010). *Logistics Management and World Seaborne Trade*. Mumbai, IND: Global Media, 2010. p 2-6.

Myatt, G. J., Johnson, W. P. (2009). *Making Sense of Data II: A Practical Guide to Data Visualization, Advanced Data Mining Methods, and Applications*. Hoboken, NJ, USA: Wiley, p 15.

Novack, R. A., & Thomas, D. J. (2004). The challenges of implementing the perfect order concept. *Transportation Journal*, 43(1), 5-16.

Prusa, P., & Tilkeridis, D. (2009). Possibilities of Logistics Policy Improvement. *Promet-Traffic & Transportation*, 21(2), 123-127.

Ramanathan, R. (2010). The moderating roles of risk and efficiency on the relationship between logistics performance and customer loyalty in e-commerce. *Transportation Research Part E-Logistics and Transportation Review*, 46(6), 950-962. doi: 10.1016/j.tre.2010.02.002

Ruamsook, K., Russell, D. M., & Thomchick, E. A. (2009). Sourcing from low-cost countries Identifying sourcing issues and prioritizing impacts on logistics performance. *International Journal of Logistics Management*, 20(1), 79-96. doi: 10.1108/09574090910954855

Saez, S. (Editor). (2010). *Directions in Development: Trade in Services Negotiations: A Guide for Developing Countries*. Herndon, VA, USA: World Bank Publications, 2010. p xi-124.

Schmitz, J., & Platts, K. W. (2004). Supplier logistics performance measurement: Indications from a study in the automotive industry. *International Journal of Production Economics*, 89(2), 231-243. doi: 10.1016/s0925-5273(02)00469-3

Shamim, M. (2009). *Encyclopaedia of Logistics Management, Volume II*. Mumbai, IND: Global Media, p 276.

Shang, K. C., & Marlow, P. B. (2005). Logistics capability and performance in Taiwan's major manufacturing firms. *Transportation Research Part E-Logistics and Transportation Review*, 41(3), 217-234. doi: 10.1016/j.tre.2004.03.002

Smith, C. D., & Mentzer, J. T. (2010). User Influence On The Relationship Between Forecast Accuracy, Application And Logistics Performance. *Journal of Business Logistics*, 31(1), 159-+.

Spindler, J. (2010). Practice/Distribution of pharmaceutical products pursuant to the 15th AMG amendment - how to combine trading and logistics performance individually. *Pharmazeutische Industrie*, 72(9), 1606-1608.

Veenstra, A., Zuidwijk, R., & van Asperen, E. (2012). The extended gate concept for container terminals: Expanding the notion of dry ports. *Maritime Economics & Logistics*, 14(1), 14-32. doi: 10.1057/mel.2011.15

Wanke, P., Arkader, R., & Hijjar, M. F. (2007). Logistics sophistication, manufacturing segments and the choice of logistics providers. *International Journal of Operations & Production Management*, 27(5), 542-559. doi: 10.1108/01443570710742401

Wood, D. F., Barone, A., Murphy, P. (2002). *International Logistics (2nd Edition)*. Saranac Lake, NY, USA: AMACOM Books, p 65-83.

World Bank (2008). *Doing Business: An Independent Evaluation: Taking the Measure of the World Bank-IFC Doing Business Indicators*. Herndon, VA, USA: World Bank Publications, p xv-51.

World Bank (2010). *Doing Business 2011: Making a Difference for Entrepreneurs*. Herndon, VA, USA: World Bank Publications, p 12-63.

World Bank (2011a). *Guide to the World Bank (3rd Edition)*. Herndon, VA, USA: World Bank Publications, p 1-2.

World Bank (2011b). *World Development Indicators: World Development Indicators 2011*. Herndon, VA, USA: World Bank Publications, p 355.

World Bank (2011c). *Doing Business 2012*. Herndon, VA, USA: World Bank Publications, p 16-17.

Yarusavage, G. (2009). 101 + Actions to Improve Transportation and Logistics Performance, 2nd Edition. *Transportation Journal*, 48(2), 63-64.

Appendix

Table A1(a). Summary statistics of economies.

Econ.	Statistic	CUST 2012	CUST 2007	INFR 2012	INFR 2007	ITRN 2012	ITRN 2007	LOGS 2012	LOGS 2007	TRAC 2012	TRAC 2007	TIME 2012	TIME 2007	OVRL 2012	OVRL 2007
World	Count	153	149	153	149	153	149	153	149	153	149	153	149	153	149
	Average	2.65	2.55	2.76	2.57	2.82	2.71	2.81	2.70	2.87	2.72	3.25	3.16	2.87	2.73
	Median	2.51	2.38	2.6	2.33	2.76	2.6	2.73	2.56	2.77	2.57	3.18	3	2.77	2.52
	Stnd. dev.	0.58	0.62	0.67	0.72	0.51	0.60	0.59	0.67	0.61	0.70	0.55	0.65	0.56	0.63
	Minimum	1.67	1.3	1.27	1.1	1.57	1.22	1.43	1.25	1.57	1	1.67	1.38	1.61	1.21
	Maximum	4.1	3.99	4.26	4.29	4.18	4.05	4.14	4.25	4.14	4.25	4.39	4.53	4.13	4.19
	Stnd. skew.	3.59	4.05	3.00	4.24	1.05	1.68	2.89	3.08	1.97	2.40	0.69	1.12	2.84	3.44
	Stnd. kurt.	-0.79	-0.45	-0.91	-0.41	-0.66	-1.16	-0.74	-0.91	-1.52	-1.16	-1.50	-1.26	-1.06	-0.74
Emerging and Developing	Count	120	117	120	117	120	117	120	117	120	117	120	117	120	117
	Average	2.44	2.31	2.52	2.29	2.65	2.50	2.59	2.45	2.66	2.47	3.07	2.93	2.66	2.49
	Median	2.38	2.25	2.47	2.25	2.67	2.50	2.62	2.41	2.59	2.41	3.02	2.88	2.60	2.42
	Stnd. dev.	0.38	0.39	0.46	0.43	0.39	0.44	0.40	0.44	0.45	0.48	0.44	0.49	0.39	0.41
	Minimum	1.67	1.3	1.27	1.1	1.57	1.22	1.43	1.25	1.57	1	1.67	1.38	1.61	1.21
	Maximum	3.61	3.52	3.84	3.8	3.59	3.68	3.74	3.67	3.83	3.71	4.1	4.12	3.78	3.73
	Stnd. skew.	2.23	2.98	1.68	3.27	-0.74	0.51	0.83	1.32	1.04	0.65	0.32	-0.12	1.52	1.89
	Stnd. kurt.	0.52	2.41	1.21	2.76	0.31	0.51	0.69	0.04	-0.16	0.35	0.14	0.48	0.77	1.77
Major Advanced Economies (G7)	Count	7	7	7	7	7	7	7	7	7	7	7	7	7	7
	Average	3.65	3.64	4.02	3.96	3.61	3.73	3.90	3.92	3.96	3.97	4.19	4.17	3.88	3.89
	Median	3.67	3.74	3.99	4.05	3.61	3.77	3.93	3.85	4	4.01	4.21	4.19	3.9	3.92
	Stnd. dev.	0.16	0.24	0.17	0.23	0.07	0.13	0.14	0.21	0.13	0.16	0.12	0.16	0.11	0.18
	Minimum	3.34	3.19	3.74	3.52	3.53	3.57	3.65	3.63	3.73	3.66	4.02	3.93	3.67	3.58
	Maximum	3.87	3.88	4.26	4.19	3.73	3.91	4.09	4.21	4.11	4.12	4.32	4.34	4.03	4.1
	Stnd. skew.	-1.07	-1.16	-0.38	-1.49	0.66	0.02	-0.68	0.12	-1.16	-1.51	-0.49	-0.45	-1.05	-0.82
	Stnd. kurt.	1.16	0.32	0.24	0.98	-0.30	-0.99	0.51	-0.58	0.40	0.92	-0.57	-0.63	1.19	0.09
European Union	Count	26	25	26	25	26	25	26	25	26	25	26	25	26	25
	Average	3.26	3.24	3.45	3.38	3.35	3.37	3.47	3.44	3.52	3.49	3.82	3.88	3.48	3.46
	Median	3.32	3.17	3.295	3.51	3.395	3.3	3.44	3.33	3.585	3.56	3.805	3.93	3.475	3.52
	Stnd. dev.	0.49	0.53	0.58	0.62	0.37	0.40	0.49	0.52	0.46	0.52	0.35	0.41	0.44	0.47
	Minimum	2.38	2.47	2.51	2.3	2.69	2.79	2.64	2.7	2.73	2.6	3.08	3.18	2.78	2.78
	Maximum	3.98	3.99	4.26	4.29	3.86	4.05	4.14	4.25	4.14	4.17	4.32	4.44	4.05	4.18
	Stnd. skew.	-0.19	0.09	-0.22	-0.31	-0.69	0.57	-0.17	0.33	-0.25	-0.22	-0.86	-0.47	-0.22	0.15
	Stnd. kurt.	-1.41	-1.67	-1.49	-1.44	-1.31	-1.39	-1.52	-1.63	-1.59	-1.57	-0.97	-1.29	-1.62	-1.66
Middle East and North Africa	Count	20	18	20	18	20	18	20	18	20	18	20	18	20	18
	Average	2.50	2.45	2.61	2.51	2.72	2.65	2.64	2.58	2.72	2.65	3.13	3.12	2.73	2.66
	Median	2.33	2.42	2.58	2.4	2.745	2.6	2.67	2.68	2.6	2.8	3.14	2.93	2.715	2.67
	Stnd. dev.	0.48	0.50	0.59	0.54	0.40	0.46	0.46	0.47	0.57	0.51	0.54	0.51	0.48	0.45
	Minimum	1.72	1.6	1.51	1.83	1.77	2	1.84	1.8	1.73	1.82	2.19	2.3	1.8	1.94
	Maximum	3.61	3.52	3.84	3.8	3.59	3.68	3.74	3.67	3.81	3.61	4.1	4.12	3.78	3.73
	Stnd. skew.	0.97	0.89	-0.03	1.51	-0.99	0.73	0.88	0.49	0.08	-0.03	0.10	1.15	0.26	0.80
	Stnd. kurt.	0.08	0.66	-0.29	0.43	1.44	0.13	0.20	0.24	-0.57	-0.74	-0.63	-0.41	0.03	0.31
Sub Saharan Africa	Count	35	36	35	36	35	36	35	36	35	36	35	36	35	36
	Average	2.27	2.19	2.30	2.12	2.49	2.36	2.43	2.31	2.42	2.29	2.86	2.75	2.47	2.33
	Median	2.29	2.205	2.31	2.13	2.5	2.33	2.42	2.32	2.39	2.235	2.77	2.735	2.48	2.295
	Stnd. dev.	0.36	0.28	0.42	0.32	0.39	0.41	0.36	0.40	0.41	0.41	0.43	0.44	0.34	0.29
	Minimum	1.67	1.58	1.27	1.4	1.57	1.67	1.43	1.67	1.57	1.6	1.67	1.83	1.61	1.77
	Maximum	3.35	3.22	3.79	3.42	3.5	3.56	3.56	3.54	3.83	3.71	4.03	3.78	3.67	3.53
	Stnd. skew.	1.76	2.26	2.05	3.63	-0.01	2.13	0.56	1.89	1.79	3.22	0.70	0.78	1.88	4.49
	Stnd. kurt.	1.39	5.33	4.64	8.66	0.83	2.30	3.10	1.31	3.50	3.61	2.10	0.22	4.67	8.71
Latin America and Caribbean	Count	21	21	21	21	21	21	21	21	21	21	21	21	21	21
	Average	2.48	2.38	2.60	2.38	2.73	2.55	2.66	2.52	2.74	2.58	3.15	3.02	2.73	2.57
	Median	2.47	2.35	2.61	2.38	2.76	2.61	2.69	2.5	2.66	2.57	3.18	3	2.75	2.55
	Stnd. dev.	0.29	0.30	0.35	0.33	0.31	0.33	0.33	0.32	0.35	0.28	0.27	0.31	0.29	0.29
	Minimum	1.78	1.95	1.78	1.78	1.94	1.8	1.74	1.95	2.14	2.16	2.67	2.5	2.03	2.05
	Maximum	3.11	3.32	3.18	3.06	3.33	3.21	3.12	3.19	3.42	3.17	3.55	3.55	3.17	3.25
	Stnd. skew.	-0.09	2.76	-0.79	0.21	-1.07	-0.36	-1.90	0.34	0.35	0.73	-0.37	-0.05	-1.01	0.73
	Stnd. kurt.	1.39	3.63	0.03	-0.26	0.93	0.17	1.31	-0.15	-0.49	-0.61	-1.09	-0.68	0.13	0.27

Table A1(b). Summary statistics of economies (continued)

Econ.	Statistic	CUST		INFR		ITRN		LOGS		TRAC		TIME		OVRL	
		2012	2007	2012	2007	2012	2007	2012	2007	2012	2007	2012	2007	2012	2007
Developing Asia	Count	18	18	18	18	18	18	18	18	18	18	18	18	18	18
	Average	2.48	2.34	2.53	2.33	2.72	2.57	2.64	2.52	2.77	2.53	3.16	2.99	2.72	2.54
	Median	2.38	2.14	2.44	2.20	2.61	2.49	2.59	2.39	2.61	2.50	3.03	3.10	2.56	2.44
	Stnd. dev.	0.39	0.51	0.48	0.54	0.44	0.53	0.47	0.56	0.46	0.59	0.45	0.57	0.42	0.53
	Minimum	1.98	1.63	1.87	1.67	1.86	1.5	1.88	1.6	1.95	1.57	2.21	2.08	2.04	1.71
	Maximum	3.28	3.36	3.61	3.33	3.46	3.36	3.47	3.4	3.54	3.51	3.86	3.95	3.52	3.48
	Stnd. skew.	1.39	0.93	1.70	1.20	0.02	-0.43	0.54	0.58	0.44	0.20	-0.22	0.07	0.87	0.60
	Stnd. kurt.	0.02	-0.79	0.37	-0.70	-0.62	-0.46	-0.65	-0.77	-0.84	-0.87	-0.32	-0.78	-0.52	-0.83
Euro Area	Count	17	16	17	16	17	16	17	16	17	16	17	16	17	16
	Average	3.32	3.35	3.58	3.54	3.43	3.41	3.56	3.55	3.61	3.60	3.86	3.97	3.56	3.56
	Median	3.40	3.38	3.74	3.62	3.53	3.38	3.65	3.59	3.67	3.65	3.88	4.04	3.67	3.56
	Stnd. dev.	0.49	0.46	0.49	0.50	0.37	0.39	0.47	0.48	0.45	0.48	0.32	0.39	0.42	0.42
	Minimum	2.38	2.61	2.79	2.68	2.69	2.85	2.76	2.77	2.84	2.84	3.23	3.25	2.83	2.92
	Maximum	3.98	3.99	4.26	4.29	4.05	4.14	4.25	4.14	4.17	4.32	4.44	4.05	4.18
	Stnd. skew.	-0.78	-0.38	-0.29	-0.37	-1.40	0.33	-0.60	-0.06	-0.76	-0.90	-0.86	-1.41	-0.79	-0.41
	Stnd. kurt.	-0.64	-1.15	-1.24	-0.98	-0.38	-1.03	-1.03	-1.10	-1.11	-0.91	-0.53	-0.26	-0.95	-0.93
Central and Eastern Europe	Count	13	12	13	12	13	12	13	12	13	12	13	12	13	12
	Average	2.72	2.51	2.83	2.53	2.94	2.82	2.91	2.72	3.01	2.67	3.46	3.20	2.98	2.74
	Median	2.71	2.50	2.62	2.49	2.97	2.86	2.91	2.85	3.07	2.73	3.56	3.39	2.99	2.83
	Stnd. dev.	0.33	0.34	0.41	0.29	0.33	0.34	0.31	0.38	0.35	0.49	0.38	0.49	0.31	0.35
	Minimum	2.24	2	2.3	2.18	2.22	2.25	2.35	2	2.41	1.67	2.79	2.13	2.45	2.08
	Maximum	3.3	3	3.62	3.12	3.47	3.31	3.52	3.29	3.54	3.27	4.04	3.69	3.51	3.15
	Stnd. skew.	0.31	0.02	0.86	1.17	-0.60	-0.47	0.44	-0.68	-0.07	-1.00	-0.67	-1.60	0.04	-0.85
	Stnd. kurt.	-0.65	-0.52	-0.61	-0.08	0.77	-0.64	0.12	-0.46	-0.62	-0.17	-0.53	0.40	-0.38	-0.56
Advanced Economies	Count	32	31	32	31	32	31	32	31	32	31	32	31	32	31
	Average	3.47	3.47	3.71	3.67	3.48	3.53	3.66	3.68	3.70	3.73	3.95	4.05	3.66	3.68
	Median	3.56	3.61	3.85	3.82	3.54	3.63	3.73	3.82	3.81	3.87	4.04	4.11	3.77	3.81
	Stnd. dev.	0.43	0.43	0.45	0.47	0.34	0.35	0.40	0.42	0.39	0.41	0.32	0.35	0.37	0.39
	Minimum	2.38	2.61	2.79	2.68	2.69	2.85	2.76	2.77	2.84	2.84	3.23	3.25	2.83	2.92
	Maximum	4.1	3.99	4.26	4.29	4.18	4.05	4.14	4.25	4.14	4.25	4.39	4.53	4.13	4.19
	Stnd. skew.	-2.12	-1.63	-1.64	-1.42	-1.21	-1.03	-1.71	-1.43	-1.93	-2.14	-1.67	-2.23	-1.88	-1.63
	Stnd. kurt.	0.38	-1.01	-1.00	-0.96	0.19	-1.06	-0.45	-0.91	-0.50	-0.05	-0.65	0.30	-0.38	-0.71
Commonwealth of Independent States	Count	11	10	11	10	11	10	11	10	11	10	11	10	11	10
	Average	2.33	2.13	2.49	2.09	2.46	2.25	2.48	2.18	2.60	2.28	2.91	2.75	2.54	2.28
	Median	2.27	2.12	2.45	2	2.58	2.24	2.4	2.14	2.58	2.3	2.87	2.73	2.56	2.3
	Stnd. dev.	0.27	0.23	0.24	0.25	0.25	0.21	0.27	0.18	0.27	0.29	0.24	0.31	0.18	0.19
	Minimum	1.92	1.91	2.03	1.78	2	2	2.14	1.9	2.13	1.67	2.51	2.11	2.28	1.93
	Maximum	2.9	2.67	2.85	2.63	2.72	2.53	2.85	2.46	3.15	2.71	3.31	3.31	2.85	2.55
	Stnd. skew.	0.86	1.87	-0.39	1.54	-1.27	0.14	0.09	0.34	0.37	-1.01	0.24	-0.40	0.25	-0.26
	Stnd. kurt.	0.70	1.80	0.14	0.83	-0.18	-1.27	-1.21	-0.55	0.61	0.89	-0.32	1.37	-0.58	-0.17
ASEAN – 5	Count	5	5	5	5	5	5	5	5	5	5	5	5	5	5
	Average	2.81	2.93	2.91	2.82	3.14	3.08	3.02	3.01	3.26	3.12	3.61	3.50	3.13	3.08
	Median	2.65	2.89	2.8	2.83	3.14	3.05	2.98	2.9	3.18	3.25	3.63	3.28	3.02	3.01
	Stnd. dev.	0.31	0.28	0.35	0.44	0.18	0.23	0.29	0.33	0.17	0.34	0.20	0.40	0.22	0.32
	Minimum	2.53	2.64	2.54	2.26	2.97	2.77	2.68	2.65	3.12	2.65	3.3	3.14	2.94	2.69
	Maximum	3.28	3.36	3.43	3.33	3.4	3.36	3.45	3.4	3.54	3.51	3.86	3.95	3.49	3.48
	Stnd. skew.	0.98	0.81	0.75	-0.12	0.57	-0.22	0.55	0.29	1.37	-0.47	-0.63	0.50	1.35	0.17
	Stnd. kurt.	-0.05	0.16	-0.13	-0.89	-0.25	-0.22	0.07	-1.16	0.88	-0.52	1.00	-1.46	0.84	-0.71
Other Advanced Economies	Count	11	11	11	11	11	11	11	11	11	11	11	11	11	11
	Average	3.64	3.57	3.79	3.72	3.51	3.63	3.72	3.76	3.74	3.81	3.99	4.12	3.73	3.76
	Median	3.6	3.76	3.86	3.82	3.46	3.67	3.71	3.82	3.79	3.76	4.05	4.11	3.73	3.81
	Stnd. dev.	0.33	0.42	0.38	0.43	0.36	0.28	0.30	0.36	0.29	0.31	0.33	0.34	0.31	0.34
	Minimum	2.95	2.73	2.96	3	3.01	3.06	3.25	3	3.17	3.27	3.4	3.56	3.14	3.13
	Maximum	4.1	3.97	4.15	4.27	4.18	4.04	4.14	4.21	4.1	4.25	4.39	4.53	4.13	4.19
	Stnd. skew.	-0.79	-1.54	-1.54	-0.86	0.58	-1.09	-0.07	-1.53	-0.77	-0.30	-1.05	-0.78	-0.60	-1.16
	Stnd. kurt.	0.42	0.04	0.43	-0.39	-0.09	0.38	-0.78	0.63	-0.01	-0.67	-0.42	-0.48	-0.26	-0.12

Table A2. Country names of economies.

Advanced Economies	
Australia, Austria, Belgium, Canada, Cyprus, Czech Republic, Denmark, Estonia, Finland, France, Germany, Greece, Hong Kong SAR, Iceland, Ireland, Israel, Italy, Japan, Korea, Luxembourg, Malta, Netherlands, New Zealand, Norway, Portugal, San Marino, Singapore, Slovak Republic, Slovenia, Spain, Sweden, Switzerland, Taiwan Province of China, United Kingdom, United States	
Euro Area	
Austria, Belgium, Cyprus, Estonia, Finland, France, Germany, Greece, Ireland, Italy, Luxembourg, Malta, Netherlands, Portugal, Slovak Republic, Slovenia, Spain	
Major Advanced Economies (G7)	
Canada, France, Germany, Italy, Japan, United Kingdom, United States	
Other Advanced Economies (Advanced Economies excluding G7 and Euro Area)	
Australia, Czech Republic, Denmark, Hong Kong SAR, Iceland, Israel, Korea, New Zealand, Norway, Singapore, San Marino, Sweden, Switzerland, Taiwan Province of China	
European Union	
Austria, Belgium, Bulgaria, Cyprus, Czech Republic, Denmark, Estonia, Finland, France, Germany, Greece, Hungary, Ireland, Italy, Latvia, Lithuania, Luxembourg, Malta, Netherlands, Poland, Portugal, Romania, Slovak Republic, Slovenia, Spain, Sweden, United Kingdom	
Emerging and Developing Economies	
Afghanistan, Albania, Algeria, Angola, Antigua and Barbuda, Argentina, Armenia, Azerbaijan, The Bahamas, Bahrain, Bangladesh, Barbados, Belarus, Belize, Benin, Bhutan, Bolivia, Bosnia and Herzegovina, Botswana, Brazil, Brunei Darussalam, Bulgaria, Burkina Faso, Burundi, Cambodia, Cameroon, Cape Verde, Central African Republic, Chad, Chile, China, Colombia, Comoros, Democratic Republic of the Congo, Republic of Congo, Costa Rica, Côte d'Ivoire, Croatia, Djibouti, Dominica, Dominican Republic, Ecuador, Egypt, El Salvador, Equatorial Guinea, Eritrea, Ethiopia, Fiji, Gabon, The Gambia, Georgia, Ghana, Grenada, Guatemala, Guinea, Guinea-Bissau, Guyana, Haiti, Honduras, Hungary, India, Indonesia, Iran, Iraq, Jamaica, Jordan, Kazakhstan, Kenya, Kiribati, Kosovo, Kuwait, Kyrgyz Republic, Lao P.D.R., Latvia, Lebanon, Lesotho, Liberia, Libya, Lithuania, FYR Macedonia, Madagascar, Malawi, Malaysia, Maldives, Mali, Marshall Islands, Mauritania, Mauritius, Mexico, Micronesia, Moldova, Mongolia, Montenegro, Morocco, Mozambique, Myanmar, Namibia, Nepal, Nicaragua, Niger, Nigeria, Oman, Pakistan, Panama, Papua New Guinea, Paraguay, Peru, Philippines, Poland, Qatar, Romania, Russia, Rwanda, Samoa, São Tomé and Príncipe, Saudi Arabia, Senegal, Serbia, Seychelles, Sierra Leone, Solomon Islands, South Africa, South Sudan, Sri Lanka, St. Kitts and Nevis, St. Lucia, St. Vincent and the Grenadines, Sudan, Suriname, Swaziland, Syria, Tajikistan, Tanzania, Thailand, Timor-Leste, Togo, Tonga, Trinidad and Tobago, Tunisia, Turkey, Turkmenistan, Tuvalu, Uganda, Ukraine, United Arab Emirates, Uruguay, Uzbekistan, Vanuatu, Venezuela, Vietnam, Yemen, Zambia, Zimbabwe	
Central and Eastern Europe	
Albania, Bosnia and Herzegovina, Bulgaria, Croatia, Hungary, Kosovo, Latvia, Lithuania, FYR Macedonia, Montenegro, Poland, Romania, Serbia, Turkey	
Commonwealth of Independent States	
Armenia, Azerbaijan, Belarus, Georgia, Kazakhstan, Kyrgyz Republic, Moldova, Russia, Tajikistan, Turkmenistan, Ukraine, Uzbekistan	
Developing Asia	
Bangladesh, Bhutan, Brunei Darussalam, Cambodia, China, Fiji, India, Indonesia, Kiribati, Lao P.D.R., Malaysia, Maldives, Marshall Islands, Micronesia, Mongolia, Myanmar, Nepal, Papua New Guinea, Philippines, Samoa, Solomon Islands, Sri Lanka, Thailand, Timor-Leste, Tonga, Tuvalu, Vanuatu, Vietnam	
ASEAN-5	
Indonesia, Malaysia, Philippines, Thailand, and Vietnam	
Latin America and the Caribbean	
Antigua and Barbuda, Argentina, The Bahamas, Barbados, Belize, Bolivia, Brazil, Chile, Colombia, Costa Rica, Dominica, Dominican Republic, Ecuador, El Salvador, Grenada, Guatemala, Guyana, Haiti, Honduras, Jamaica, Mexico, Nicaragua, Panama, Paraguay, Peru, St. Kitts and Nevis, St. Lucia, St. Vincent and the Grenadines, Suriname, Trinidad and Tobago, Uruguay, Venezuela	
Middle East, North Africa, Afghanistan, and Pakistan	
Afghanistan, Algeria, Bahrain, Djibouti, Egypt, Iran, Iraq, Jordan, Kuwait, Lebanon, Libya, Mauritania, Morocco, Oman, Pakistan, Qatar, Saudi Arabia, Sudan, Syria, Tunisia, United Arab Emirates, Yemen	
Middle East and North Africa	
Algeria, Bahrain, Djibouti, Egypt, Iran, Iraq, Jordan, Kuwait, Lebanon, Libya, Mauritania, Morocco, Oman, Qatar, Saudi Arabia, Sudan, Syria, Tunisia, United Arab Emirates, Yemen	
Sub-Saharan Africa	
Angola, Benin, Botswana, Burkina Faso, Burundi, Cameroon, Cape Verde, Central African Republic, Chad, Comoros, Democratic Republic of the Congo, Republic of Congo, Côte d'Ivoire, Equatorial Guinea, Eritrea, Ethiopia, Gabon, The Gambia, Ghana, Guinea, Guinea-Bissau, Kenya, Lesotho, Liberia, Madagascar, Malawi, Mali, Mauritius, Mozambique, Namibia, Niger, Nigeria, Rwanda, São Tomé and Príncipe, Senegal, Seychelles, Sierra Leone, South Africa, South Sudan, Swaziland, Tanzania, Togo, Uganda, Zambia, Zimbabwe	

Table A3. The result of clustering of customs clearance process (CUST)

Cluster	Countries
1	Azerbaijan, Burundi, Chad, Congo, Rep., Djibouti, Eritrea, Haiti, Iraq, Sierra Leone
2	Burkina Faso, Comoros, Congo, Dem. Rep., Cuba, Ethiopia, Fiji, Gabon, Iran, Islamic Rep., Jamaica, Kenya, Lebanon, Lesotho, Liberia, Libya, Moldova, Mongolia, Nepal, Nigeria, Papua New Guinea, Russian Federation, Rwanda, Sudan, Tanzania, Venezuela, RB
3	Afghanistan, Albania, Algeria, Angola, Argentina, Armenia, Belarus, Benin, Bhutan, Bolivia, Brazil, Cambodia, Cameroon, Costa Rica, Cote d'Ivoire, Dominican Republic, Ecuador, Egypt, Arab Rep., El Salvador, Estonia, Gambia, The, Ghana, Greece, Guinea, Guinea-Bissau, Guyana, Honduras, Indonesia, Jordan, Kazakhstan, Kyrgyz Republic, Lao PDR, Macedonia, FYR, Malawi, Maldives, Mauritania, Mauritius, Montenegro, Myanmar, Panama, Paraguay, Sao Tome and Principe, Senegal, Serbia, Solomon Islands, Sri Lanka, Syrian Arab Republic, Tajikistan, Togo, Ukraine, Uzbekistan, Yemen, Rep., Zimbabwe
4	Bahamas, The, Bahrain, Bosnia and Herzegovina, Botswana, Bulgaria, Chile, Colombia, Croatia, Cyprus, Czech Republic, Georgia, Guatemala, Hungary, India, Kuwait, Latvia, Lithuania, Madagascar, Malta, Mexico, Morocco, Namibia, Niger, Oman, Pakistan, Peru, Philippines, Portugal, Qatar, Romania, Saudi Arabia, Slovak Republic, Slovenia, Thailand, Tunisia, Turkey, Uruguay, Vietnam
5	Australia, Austria, Belgium, Canada, China, Denmark, Finland, France, Germany, Hong Kong SAR, China, Iceland, Ireland, Italy, Japan, Korea, Rep., Luxembourg, Malaysia, Netherlands, New Zealand, Norway, Poland, Singapore, South Africa, Spain, Sweden, Switzerland, United Arab Emirates, United Kingdom, United States

Table A4. The result of clustering of quality of trade and transport-related infrastructure (INFR)

Cluster	Countries
1	Afghanistan, Algeria, Burundi, Chad, Comoros, Congo, Dem. Rep., Congo, Rep., Cuba, Djibouti, Eritrea, Gabon, Gambia, The, Ghana, Guyana, Haiti, Iraq, Kenya, Lesotho, Libya, Myanmar, Nepal, Rwanda, Solomon Islands, Sudan, Tajikistan, Venezuela, RB
2	Albania, Angola, Armenia, Azerbaijan, Benin, Bhutan, Bolivia, Burkina Faso, Cambodia, Cameroon, Colombia, Costa Rica, Cote d'Ivoire, Dominican Republic, Ecuador, El Salvador, Ethiopia, Fiji, Guatemala, Guinea, Guinea-Bissau, Honduras, Indonesia, Iran, Islamic Rep., Jamaica, Jordan, Kazakhstan, Kyrgyz Republic, Lao PDR, Latvia, Lebanon, Liberia, Lithuania, Macedonia, FYR, Madagascar, Maldives, Mauritania, Moldova, Mongolia, Montenegro, Namibia, Niger, Nigeria, Pakistan, Papua New Guinea, Paraguay, Peru, Romania, Russian Federation, Sao Tome and Principe, Senegal, Serbia, Sierra Leone, Sri Lanka, Syrian Arab Republic, Tanzania, Togo, Ukraine, Uzbekistan, Vietnam, Yemen, Rep., Zimbabwe
3	Argentina, Bahamas, The, Bahrain, Belarus, Bosnia and Herzegovina, Botswana, Brazil, Bulgaria, Chile, Croatia, Cyprus, Czech Republic, Egypt, Arab Rep., Estonia, Georgia, Greece, Hungary, Iceland, India, Ireland, Kuwait, Malawi, Malaysia, Malta, Mauritius, Mexico, Morocco, New Zealand, Oman, Panama, Philippines, Poland, Portugal, Qatar, Saudi Arabia, Slovak Republic, Slovenia, Thailand, Tunisia, Uruguay
4	Australia, Austria, Belgium, Canada, China, Denmark, Finland, France, Germany, Hong Kong SAR, China, Italy, Japan, Korea, Rep., Luxembourg, Netherlands, Norway, Singapore, South Africa, Spain, Sweden, Switzerland, Turkey, United Arab Emirates, United Kingdom, United States

Table A5. The result of clustering of ease of arranging competitively priced shipments (ITRN)

Cluster	Countries
1	Burundi
2	Chad, Comoros, Congo, Rep., Cuba, Djibouti, Haiti, Kyrgyz Republic, Lesotho, Moldova, Mongolia, Nepal, Sierra Leone, Sudan
3	Afghanistan, Angola, Azerbaijan, Benin, Botswana, Burkina Faso, Cameroon, Congo, Dem. Rep., Ethiopia, Fiji, Gabon, Guyana, Iran, Islamic Rep., Iraq, Jamaica, Lao PDR, Madagascar, Maldives, Mauritania, Mauritius, Montenegro, Myanmar, Namibia, Papua New Guinea, Paraguay, Rwanda, Sao Tome and Principe, Solomon Islands, Tajikistan, Uzbekistan
4	Albania, Algeria, Armenia, Bahamas, The, Bahrain, Belarus, Bhutan, Bolivia, Cambodia, Colombia, Costa Rica, Dominican Republic, El Salvador, Eritrea, Estonia, Gambia, The, Georgia, Ghana, Greece, Guatemala, Guinea, Guinea-Bissau, Honduras, India, Kenya, Kuwait, Latvia, Lebanon, Liberia, Libya, Macedonia, FYR, Nigeria, Oman, Panama, Russian Federation, Senegal, Serbia, Slovak Republic, Syrian Arab Republic, Ukraine, Venezuela, RB, Zimbabwe
5	Bosnia and Herzegovina, Brazil, Bulgaria, Chile, Cote d'Ivoire, Croatia, Cyprus, Czech Republic, Ecuador, Egypt, Arab Rep., Hungary, Iceland, India, Indonesia, Jordan, Lithuania, Malawi, Malta, Mexico, Morocco, New Zealand, Niger, Pakistan, Peru, Philippines, Qatar, Romania, Saudi Arabia, Sri Lanka, Tanzania, Thailand, Togo, Tunisia, Uruguay, Vietnam, Yemen, Rep.
6	Argentina, Australia, Austria, Belgium, Canada, China, Denmark, Finland, France, Germany, Hong Kong SAR, China, Ireland, Italy, Japan, Korea, Rep., Luxembourg, Malaysia, Netherlands, Norway, Poland, Portugal, Singapore, Slovenia, South Africa, Spain, Sweden, Switzerland, Turkey, United Arab Emirates, United Kingdom, United States

Table A6. The result of clustering of quality of logistics services (LOGS)

Cluster	Countries
1	Burundi
2	Angola, Chad, Djibouti, Eritrea, Haiti, Mongolia, Sierra Leone
3	Afghanistan, Algeria, Azerbaijan, Burkina Faso, Comoros, Congo, Dem. Rep., Congo, Rep., Cuba, Ethiopia, Fiji, Iraq, Jamaica, Jordan, Kyrgyz Republic, Libya, Mauritania, Moldova, Nepal, Papua New Guinea, Rwanda, Solomon Islands, Tajikistan, Togo, Zimbabwe
4	Armenia, Bhutan, Cambodia, Cameroon, Costa Rica, Gabon, Gambia, The, Guyana, Honduras, Kenya, Lao PDR, Lebanon, Lesotho, Liberia, Montenegro, Myanmar, Niger, Nigeria, Paraguay, Sao Tome and Principe, Senegal, Sudan, Syrian Arab Republic, Uzbekistan, Venezuela, RB
5	Albania, Bahamas, The, Belarus, Bolivia, Botswana, Cote d'Ivoire, Dominican Republic, Ecuador, El Salvador, Estonia, Georgia, Ghana, Greece, Guatemala, Guinea, Guinea-Bissau, Indonesia, Iran, Islamic Rep., Kazakhstan, Kuwait, Latvia, Macedonia, FYR, Madagascar, Malawi, Maldives, Mauritius, Namibia, Oman, Pakistan, Panama, Romania, Russian Federation, Serbia, Sri Lanka, Tanzania, Ukraine, Vietnam, Yemen, Rep.
6	Argentina, Bahrain, Benin, Bosnia and Herzegovina, Brazil, Bulgaria, Chile, Colombia, Croatia, Cyprus, Czech Republic, Egypt, Arab Rep., Hungary, India, Lithuania, Malta, Mexico, Morocco, New Zealand, Peru, Philippines, Poland, Qatar, Saudi Arabia, Slovak Republic, Slovenia, Thailand, Tunisia, Uruguay
7	Australia, Austria, Belgium, Canada, China, Denmark, Finland, France, Germany, Hong Kong SAR, China, Iceland, Ireland, Italy, Japan, Korea, Rep., Luxembourg, Malaysia, Netherlands, Norway, Portugal, Singapore, South Africa, Spain, Sweden, Switzerland, Turkey, United Arab Emirates, United Kingdom, United States

Table A7. The result of clustering of ability to track and trace consignments (TRAC)

Cluster	Countries
1	Burundi, Chad, Djibouti, Eritrea, Iraq, Sudan
2	Afghanistan, Angola, Burkina Faso, Comoros, Ethiopia, Gabon, Guyana, Haiti, Lesotho, Nepal, Senegal, Sierra Leone, Tajikistan
3	Algeria, Congo, Dem. Rep., Congo, Rep., Cuba, Dominican Republic, Fiji, Ghana, Guinea, Honduras, Iran, Islamic Rep., Jamaica, Kenya, Kyrgyz Republic, Lao PDR, Liberia, Libya, Macedonia, FYR, Maldives, Mauritania, Moldova, Mongolia, Myanmar, Niger, Nigeria, Papua New Guinea, Rwanda, Solomon Islands, Syrian Arab Republic, Togo, Uzbekistan, Zimbabwe
4	Albania, Armenia, Azerbaijan, Bahamas, The, Belarus, Benin, Bhutan, Bolivia, Bosnia and Herzegovina, Botswana, Cambodia, Cameroon, Colombia, Costa Rica, Cote d'Ivoire, Ecuador, Egypt, Arab Rep., El Salvador, Gambia, The, Georgia, Guatemala, Guinea-Bissau, Jordan, Kazakhstan, Lebanon, Lithuania, Madagascar, Malawi, Mauritius, Montenegro, Namibia, Oman, Pakistan, Paraguay, Russian Federation, Sao Tome and Principe, Slovak Republic, Sri Lanka, Tanzania, Venezuela, RB
5	Argentina, Bahrain, Brazil, Bulgaria, Chile, Croatia, Cyprus, Czech Republic, Estonia, Greece, Iceland, India, Indonesia, Kuwait, Latvia, Malta, Mexico, Morocco, Panama, Peru, Philippines, Poland, Romania, Saudi Arabia, Serbia, Slovenia, Thailand, Tunisia, Ukraine, Uruguay, Vietnam, Yemen, Rep.
6	Australia, Austria, Belgium, Canada, China, Denmark, Finland, France, Germany, Hong Kong SAR, China, Hungary, Ireland, Italy, Japan, Korea, Rep., Luxembourg, Malaysia, Netherlands, New Zealand, Norway, Portugal, Qatar, Singapore, South Africa, Spain, Sweden, Switzerland, Turkey, United Arab Emirates, United Kingdom, United States

Table A8. The result of clustering of frequency with which shipments reach the consignee within the scheduled time (TIME)

Cluster	Countries
1	Burundi
2	Congo, Dem. Rep., Cuba, Djibouti, Nepal, Sierra Leone, Sudan
3	Angola, Eritrea, Ethiopia, Gambia, The, Guinea, Libya, Mauritania, Myanmar, Namibia, Tajikistan
4	Afghanistan, Burkina Faso, Chad, Comoros, Ghana, Guinea-Bissau, Guyana, Haiti, Iran, Islamic Rep., Iraq, Kazakhstan, Kyrgyz Republic, Lao PDR, Lesotho, Macedonia, FYR, Moldova, Paraguay, Rwanda, Sao Tome and Principe, Senegal, Togo
5	Algeria, Bahamas, The, Belarus, Bhutan, Bolivia, Cambodia, Congo, Rep., Dominican Republic, Gabon, Georgia, Honduras, Jamaica, Jordan, Kenya, Liberia, Maldives, Mongolia, Montenegro, Nigeria, Papua New Guinea, Russian Federation, Solomon Islands, Sri Lanka, Tanzania, Uzbekistan
6	Argentina, Armenia, Azerbaijan, Cameroon, Costa Rica, Cote d'Ivoire, El Salvador, Estonia, Fiji, Greece, Guatemala, Kuwait, Latvia, Lebanon, Madagascar, Malawi, Niger, Oman, Pakistan, Philippines, Serbia, Syrian Arab Republic, Ukraine, Uruguay, Venezuela, RB, Yemen, Rep., Zimbabwe
7	Albania, Austria, Bahrain, Benin, Bosnia and Herzegovina, Botswana, Brazil, Bulgaria, Chile, China, Colombia, Croatia, Cyprus, Czech Republic, Ecuador, Egypt, Arab Rep., Hungary, Iceland, India, Indonesia, Ireland, Lithuania, Malta, Mauritius, Mexico, Morocco, New Zealand, Panama, Peru, Romania, Saudi Arabia, Slovak Republic, Slovenia, Thailand, Tunisia, Vietnam
8	Australia, Belgium, Canada, Denmark, Finland, France, Germany, Hong Kong SAR, China, Italy, Japan, Korea, Rep., Luxembourg, Malaysia, Netherlands, Norway, Poland, Portugal, Qatar, Singapore, South Africa, Spain, Sweden, Switzerland, Turkey, United Arab Emirates, United Kingdom, United States

Table A9. The result of clustering of overall logistics performance (OVRL)

Cluster	Countries
1	Burundi
2	Djibouti
3	Chad, Comoros, Congo, Rep., Eritrea, Haiti, Iraq, Nepal, Sierra Leone, Sudan
4	Afghanistan, Angola, Burkina Faso, Congo, Dem. Rep., Cuba, Ethiopia, Gabon, Guyana, Kyrgyz Republic, Lesotho, Libya, Mauritania, Moldova, Mongolia, Myanmar, Papua New Guinea, Rwanda, Tajikistan
5	Algeria, Armenia, Azerbaijan, Belarus, Bhutan, Bolivia, Cambodia, Cameroon, El Salvador, Fiji, Gambia, The, Ghana, Guinea, Guinea-Bissau, Honduras, Iran, Islamic Rep., Jamaica, Jordan, Kenya, Lao PDR, Lebanon, Liberia, Macedonia, FYR, Maldives, Montenegro, Nigeria, Paraguay, Russian Federation, Sao Tome and Principe, Senegal, Solomon Islands, Syrian Arab Republic, Togo, Uzbekistan, Venezuela, RB, Zimbabwe
6	Albania, Bahamas, The, Benin, Botswana, Colombia, Costa Rica, Cote d'Ivoire, Dominican Republic, Ecuador, Estonia, Georgia, Greece, Guatemala, Kazakhstan, Kuwait, Latvia, Madagascar, Malawi, Mauritius, Namibia, Niger, Oman, Pakistan, Serbia, Sri Lanka, Tanzania, Ukraine, Yemen, Rep.
7	Argentina, Bahrain, Bosnia and Herzegovina, Brazil, Chile, Croatia, Czech Republic, Egypt, Arab Rep., Hungary, India, Indonesia, Lithuania, Malta, Mexico, Morocco, Panama, Peru, Philippines, Romania, Slovak Republic, Tunisia, Uruguay, Vietnam
8	Bulgaria, China, Cyprus, Iceland, Ireland, Malaysia, New Zealand, Poland, Portugal, Qatar, Saudi Arabia, Slovenia, Thailand, Turkey
9	Australia, Austria, Belgium, Canada, Denmark, Finland, France, Germany, Hong Kong SAR, China, Italy, Japan, Korea, Rep., Luxembourg, Netherlands, Norway, Singapore, South Africa, Spain, Sweden, Switzerland, United Arab Emirates, United Kingdom, United States

Chapter 2. The performances of logistics services in developed and developing countries: A review and cluster analysis

Abstract. As supply chains are so varied and complex, logistics performance depends on many factors, such as services, investment and policies. Infrastructure construction, the development of regulatory regimes for transport services and the design and implementation of efficient customs clearance procedures are all areas in which governments play an important role. Improvements in global logistics are also being driven by innovation and increases in global trade. This study analyzes the perceptions of countries' logistics efficiencies by using various measures drawn from the World Bank database. It further investigates correlations among logistics performance indicators and the relationships between these and GDP per capita and the World Bank's 'doing business' scores through regression analysis. In addition, cluster analysis is performed on the logistics performance indicators to group similar countries. The presented findings show that GDP plays an important role in determining a country's logistics performance. Bidirectional relationships between all logistics performance indicators and GDP are also demonstrated. In addition, the study shows that countries' doing business scores correlate with all pairs of logistics performance scores as well as with GDP.

Keywords: logistics performance, policy, transportation, trade facilitation, lagging regions, landlocked, developed and developing, cluster analysis

1. Introduction

The lasting impact of the Asian financial crisis in 1997, the deterioration of the global economy following the bursting of the dotcom bubble in 2001, the financial tsunami in 2008 and the ever-increasing demand for better services have all contributed to the decline in margins for all companies in the world (Lai and Cheng 2009). To cope with these challenges, many companies are looking for ways to strengthen and preserve their market positions (Lai and Cheng 2009). Increasingly sophisticated global market demand is forcing companies to formulate intelligent strategies, including the use of international logistics techniques to gain competitive advantage in the management of supply chains (Wood *et al.* 2002). Logistics is therefore becoming increasingly popular as a competitive weapon for companies to gain a cost advantage and provide added-value services (Lai and Cheng 2009).

Logistics activities are interdependent, require the allocation of resources to achieve service goals and reduce waste in the supply chain such as idle time and the duplication of effort (Lai *et al.* 2008). The rise of emerging economies has been marked by a change in transport and logistics integration functions along the supply chain, notably the functions of seaports (Ng *et al.* 2012). Institutional reforms have also improved the management of port operations (Ng *et al.* 2012). Moreover, owing to technological improvements, rapid delivery is fully expected to shippers and shipments aim to spend a minimum time in seaports, thereby reducing costs (Ng *et al.* 2012).

This logistics revolution has undoubtedly increased both production efficiency and the distribution of goods. Products are manufactured to respond to specific consumers' requests and are then delivered with greater speed, accuracy and cost. It can be argued that these changes have created a win/win situation for all parties in the supply chain. Companies have reduced their costs and improved their levels of profitability, allowing them to become more competitive by offering consumers the products they want when they want them, and often at a lower price (Bonacich and Wilson 2008). Because collaboration is essential in such an increasingly demanding business environment, the successful companies of tomorrow will be those that manage their supply chains more strategically, creating new revenue opportunities, efficiency and customer loyalty (Ireland 2004).

Relationships between transport and the economy are highly complex and poorly understood. Transport is a massive undertaking with significant direct and indirect effects on productivity and economic growth (Norwood 2002). Industries, transportation, transportation services, vehicle manufacturing and infrastructure construction are the main economic activities in this regard (Norwood 2002). Indeed, transport costs are, to a greater or lesser degree, incurred by most goods and services in the economy (Norwood 2002). However, transport is an enabler of both economic activity and international trade. Transportation can even serve as a measure of economic activity in many cases; for example, it can be a leading indicator, since physical movements precede financial transactions (Norwood 2002).

Developing countries spend a much higher proportion of GDP on transport and logistics than developed countries (Brar *et al.* 2010). Moreover, previous studies have demonstrated the connection between logistics performance and economic development (e.g. Arvis *et al.* 2007, Hummels 2000, Wilson *et al.* 2003, de Souza *et al.* 2007, Balestreri *et al.* 2009). This leads to a number of outstanding questions regarding the logistics–performance relation. For example, as far as logistics infrastructure, regulatory regimes for transport services and the design and implementation of customs clearance procedures are concerned, can the GDP per capita of a country successfully predict logistics performance in developing and developed countries? Is it possible to predict logistics performance from GDP figures and the World Bank's 'doing business' (DB) scores, and vice versa? How strongly is GDP linked to various logistics performance aspects? What are the key logistics performance areas on which government policies need to focus in order to increase outcomes?

The remainder of this study is organized as follows. Section 2 reviews the literature on logistics performance. Section 3 introduces the data and methods used for the analyses of the perceptions of countries' logistics efficiencies by using various measures drawn from the World Bank database. It further investigates correlations among logistics performance indicators and the relationships between these and GDP per capita and DB scores through regression analysis. In addition, cluster analysis is performed on the logistics performance indicators to group similar countries based on the choice of clustering algorithm. Section 4 presents and discusses the empirical findings. The study is concluded in Section 5.

2. Literature review

Logistics is the science of managing and controlling the flow of goods, energy, information and other resources such as products, services and people from the source of production to the market (Goldsby and Martichenko 2005). As acknowledged by Lowe (2002), logistics covers the total concept of planning and organizing the supply and circulation of materials and supplies from the original source through the stages of production, assembly, packaging, storage, handling and distribution to the final consumer.

The formulation of transport policy, as expressed by Van Geenhuizen *et al.* (2007), has become a more complex task over recent decades. Transport is not pursued for itself, but is rather derived from other activities such as living, working, production and recreation, which are themselves subject to greater complexity (Van Geenhuizen *et al.* 2007). Modern lifestyles and innovative production methods generate increased demand for transport, including higher frequencies of services and longer routes (Van Geenhuizen *et al.* 2007). As argued by Lowe (2002), it is difficult, or almost impossible, to trade internationally, carry out global export/import processes, reposition raw materials/products and manufacture final products without professional logistics support.

Shamim (2009) highlighted that the operational responsibility of logistics is the geographical repositioning of raw materials, work in process and finished goods inventory as needed, at the lowest cost possible. A wide range of third-party suppliers provides logistics and supply chain support (Shamim 2009). Van Geenhuizen *et al.* (2007) suggested that while new technologies help make transport systems more powerful and effective at the same time, they also introduce additional challenges because of reliability problems and feedback effects. Further, as acknowledged by Van Geenhuizen *et al.* (2007), another reason for the increasing complexity is the many often contradictory objectives involved in the determination of transport policy. These objectives include to increase network capacity in order to accommodate higher flow rates, to reduce costs and to minimize environmental impacts.

Hausman *et al.* (2012) highlighted that global trade is an important element of economic development in the world economy. Countries depend on trade to increase their sales of domestic products in world markets, while in emerging economies trade is an important tool for economic development (Hausman *et al.* 2012). Brar *et al.* (2010) pointed out that the rapidly changing literature on trade logistics and transport has, unsurprisingly, focused on the international dimensions of logistics. For instance, previous studies have shown that landlocked countries face particular challenges when linking global supply chains that result from the long distances to seaports and need to cross borders (Brar *et al.* 2010). For example, it has been found that distance to a seaport negatively affects the economic performance of a geographical area (Krugman 1991, Gallup *et al.* 1998, MacKellar *et al.* 2000). In addition, owing to higher logistics costs and lower global economic integration, the volume of trade between landlocked countries is smaller than that between non-landlocked nations (Limao and Venables 2001). The costs of crossing borders are also generally high, while the existence of a border often requires infrastructure costs if the transport corridors on either side are not well coordinated (Hausmann 2001, Raballand 2003, Teravaninthorn and Raballand 2008).

The solutions to transport-related problems are constantly changing as the prevailing technological, economic and political decision-making contexts improve (Van Geenhuizen *et al.* 2007). As noted by Hausman *et al.* (2012), the trade volume between two countries depends on the attractiveness of the requirements between the exporting and the importing parties. When an importing country has several sources of supply, the distance and cost of crossing borders, freight charges and customs duties collected become important determinants of the bilateral trade volume between trading partners (Hausman *et al.* 2012). Van Geenhuizen *et al.* (2007) also acknowledged that the new European network, following the recent inclusion of countries that have good access to new spatial positions and functional networks (and the benefits associated with their use) is considered to be a critical success factor for the development of regions, cities and businesses (Van Geenhuizen *et al.* 2007).

Krugman (1991) argued that external economies of scale can be achieved at the local as well as at the national and international levels (see also Brar *et al.* 2010). However, it is important to understand the factors that lead to increased competitiveness at the local level and, in this respect, sensitivity to geography is important (Brar *et al.* 2010). Without serious efforts to improve logistics and transport systems at this level, few actors in developing countries will be able to take advantage of the opportunities offered by globalization (e.g. lower barriers to trade; Brar *et al.* 2010). The key question in this vein is how small producers can organize themselves to overcome the obstacle of distance in a way that allows them to connect to national and global supply chains (Brar *et al.* 2010).

Table 1. Highlighted studies about issues that affect logistics performance.

Field of study	Authors
Logistics and economic development	Arvis *et al.* (2007), Hummels (2000), Wilson *et al.* (2003), Gannon and Liu (1997), Banomyong *et al.* (2008), de Souza *et al.* (2007), Balestreri *et al.* (2009), Dollar *et al.* (2004)
Trade costs, trade barriers	Marques-Ramos *et al.* (2011), Hoekman and Nicita (2010), Henderson *et al.* (2001), Krugman (1991), Subramanian *et al.* (2005), de Groot *et al.* (2004)
Transport costs, infrastructure	Marquez *et al.* (2007), Limao and Venables (2001), Nordas and Piermartini (2004), Keil and Young (2008), Subramanian and Arnold (2001), Clark *et al.* (2004)
Ports, maritime costs, efficiency	Martinez-Zarzoso *et al.* (2008), Wilmsmeier *et al.* (2006), Wilson *et al.* (2005), Clark *et al.* (2004), Hausman (2004)
Trade facilitation	Moïsé *et al.* (2011), Iwanow and Kirkpatrick (2009), Behar and Manner (2008), Wilson and Otsuki (2007), Soloaga *et al.* (2006), Dennis (2006), Decreux and Fontagne (2006), Hummels (2001)

In this context, accessibility plays a fundamental role in the investigation of the slow dynamics typical of supply networks (e.g. infrastructure, equipment/location development) and the fast dynamics characteristic of the user side (e.g. demand for mobility/communication model) (Van Geenhuizen *et al.* 2007). For instance, Brar *et al.* (2010) reported that unless small farmers have access to efficient logistics services, they are excluded from global supply chains. Moreover, during the recent financial crisis, some companies in the developed world shortened their supply chains. Brar *et al.* (2010) found that more than a quarter of businesses in North America and Europe that use third-party logistics providers have reduced their supply chains as well as their stocks. Further, they pointed out that when companies have minimum buffers, they have little room for errors in the management of their supply chains and must rely on the agility of suppliers agile. The authors also found that this constraint could exclude producers in low-income countries that do not usually have access to efficient logistics services.

Transportation-related infrastructure such as roads, bridges, tunnels, railways, canals, seaports and airports is a cornerstone of modern economics (Underhill 2010). Transport, in this respect, has a major impact on the economic and spatial development of cities and regions. Indeed, the attractiveness of particular locations depends in part on their relative accessibility and quality and quantity of their transport infrastructure (Banister, 1995). It has always been assumed that a high-quality transport infrastructure is a prerequisite for economic development, but this hypothesis has never been studied in depth (Banister and Berechman 1999).

Research shows that transport infrastructure has the greatest impact at the firm level in terms of external costs (Brar *et al.* 2010). Improving connectivity through the provision of appropriate services can reduce the effect of tariff barriers for countries that are a long distance from major markets (Brar *et al.* 2010). Further, there is a virtuous circle between transport costs and trade, namely as trade increases, the cost of transport reduces (Brar *et al.* 2010). Therefore, increases in local interactions and reductions in economic distances within a country and across the world contribute to this virtuous circle (Brar *et al.* 2010). Table 1 highlights previous studies about infrastructure, regulatory regimes for transport services and customs in relation to trade facilitation, economic development and trade and transport costs.

This study mainly differs from the existing literature in that it analyzes correlations among logistics performance indicators and GDP per capita and DB scores. Moreover, it clusters logistics indicators with the help of algorithm's decision, which indicates the connections between economic development and logistics performance, and presents policy recommendations for achieving higher logistics performance.

3. Data and methods

Until recently, policymakers and stakeholders in the private sector had no baseline data for identifying business constraints or creating constituencies for reform. In this regard, data on trade facilitation and logistics performance were rare; however, the Logistics Performance Index (LPI) has now filled this gap (Arnold *et al.* 2010). By providing comprehensive data on country-level performance and a general idea of any problems, the LPI helps raise awareness of and increases dialogue between policymakers and the private sector on logistical bottlenecks and reform priorities to facilitate international trade and transport at the national and sub-regional levels (Arnold *et al.* 2010).

Surveys of logistics performance are conducted by the World Bank in partnership with academic and international institutions, private companies and individuals engaged in international logistics. The LPI assesses logistics performance in six environmental aspects (see Definitions), based on more than 5,000 country assessments by nearly 1,000 international freight forwarders. In this way, it reflects the perceptions of a country's logistics based on the following six dimensions: (1) the efficiency of the clearance process, (2) quality of trade and transport-related infrastructure, (3) ease of organizing expeditions at competitive prices, (4) quality of logistics services, (5) ability to track and trace shipments, and (6) frequency with which shipments reach the consignee within the time limit.

Respondents evaluate eight markets on these six core dimensions using a five-point scale from 1 (worst) to 5 (best). The target markets are chosen randomly based on the most important export and import markets of the respondent's country as well as for landlocked countries and neighboring countries that connect them to international markets. The scores for the six dimensions are then averaged for all respondents and aggregated into a single score (World Bank, 2010).

The LPI also summarizes the following seven areas of performance based on the same five-point scale: (i) the effectiveness and efficiency of the clearance process by customs and other border control agencies, (ii) the quality of transport infrastructure and IT for logistics, (iii) the ease and affordability of organizing expeditions, (iv) competence in the local logistics industry (e.g. transport operators and customs brokers), (v) the ability to track and trace shipments, (vi) internal logistics costs (e.g., local transportation costs) and (vii) terminal handling and storage (World Bank

2008). In addition, the DB project, one of the products of the knowledge gathered by the World Bank, is an annual benchmarking program first published in 2004. The DB project provides objective measures of business regulations and their enforcement in 183 countries and selected cities at the sub-national and regional levels. The goal of the project is to provide an objective basis for understanding and improving the regulatory environment for businesses worldwide.

This section next investigates correlations among these indicators and applies a regression model in order to examine how each LPI indicator influences the others. Statistical relationships between GDP per capita, the LPI indicators and the overall DB scores are also shown. In addition, a cluster analysis is performed on the overall LPI indicators to visualize countries' relative positioning.

3.1 Correlations and regression analysis

Table 2 shows the correlations between each pair of variables. These correlation coefficients range between -1 and +1 and measure the strength of the linear relationships between these variables. The second number in each location of the table is the p-value, which tests the statistical significance of the estimated correlations. P-values below 0.05 indicate statistically significant non-zero correlations at the 95% confidence level. All pairs of variables have p-values below 0.05. Thus, all correlations are significant at $p < 0.05$ with N=161 (casewise deletion of missing data).

Table 2. Correlations between each pair of variables.

	GDP	CUST	INFR	ITRN	LOGS	TIME	TRAC	OVRL
GDP	1	.77	.80	.61	.74	.68	.73	.77
	-	p=0.00	p=0.00	p=.000	p=0.00	p=0.00	p=0.00	p=0.00
CUST	.77	1	.94	.76	.93	.84	.88	.96
	p=0.00	-	p=0.00	p=0.00	p=0.00	p=0.00	p=0.00	p=0.00
INFR	.80	.94	1	.78	.95	.85	.90	.97
	p=0.00	p=0.00	-	p=0.00	p=0.00	p=0.00	p=0.00	p=0.00
ITRN	.61	.76	.78	1	.77	.69	.76	.84
	p=.000	p=0.00	p=0.00	-	p=0.00	p=0.00	p=0.00	p=0.00
LOGS	.74	.93	.95	.77	1	.86	.92	.97
	p=0.00	p=0.00	p=0.00	p=0.00	-	p=0.00	p=0.00	p=0.00
TIME	.68	.84	.85	.69	.86	1	.83	.90
	p=0.00	p=0.00	p=0.00	p=0.00	p=0.00	-	p=0.00	p=0.00
TRAC	.73	.88	.90	.76	.92	.83	1	.94
	p=0.00	p=0.00	p=0.00	p=0.00	p=0.00	p=0.00	-	p=0.00
OVRL	.77	.96	.97	.84	.97	.90	.94	1
	p=0.00	p=0.00	p=0.00	p=0.00	p=0.00	p=0.00	p=0.00	-

gross domestic product per capita (GDP)
customs clearance process (CUST)
quality of trade and transport-related infrastructure (INFR)
ease of arranging competitively priced shipments (ITRN)
quality of logistics services (LOGS)
ability to track and trace consignments (TRAC)
frequency with which shipments reach the consignee within the scheduled time (TIME)
overall logistics performance (OVRL)

The pairs of variables with positive correlation coefficients and p-values below 0.05 tend to increase together. For the pairs with negative correlation coefficients and p-values below 0.05, one variable tends to decrease while the other increases (see Figure 1). For pairs with p-values greater than 0.05, there is no significant relationship between the two variables.

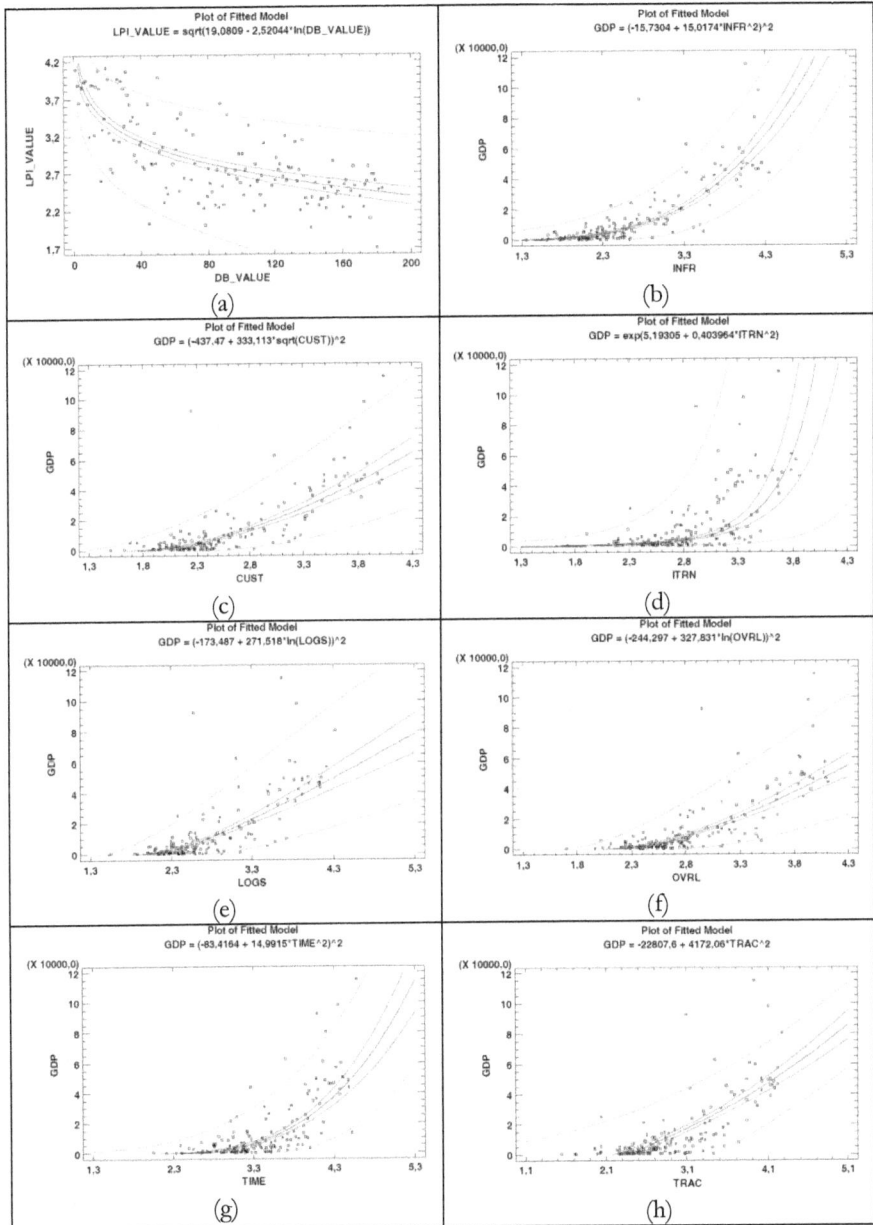

Figure 1. Regression models with the best fittings. (a) LPI vs. DB, (b) GDP vs. INF, (c) GDP vs. CUST, (d) GDP vs. ITRN, (e) GDP vs. LOGS, (f) GDP vs. OVRL, (g) GDP vs. TIME, (h) GDP vs. TRAC

The results of the fitting models describe the relationships between pairs (see Table 3). The equations of the fitted model are also shown in Table 3.

Table 3. The coefficients and best-fitted regression models.

Pairs	Parameter	Least Squares Est.	Stnd. Error	T Stat.	The best fitted regression model	Actual model
LPI vs. DB	Intercept	19.08	0.78	24.42	Squared-Y logarithmic-X model: Y = sqrt(a + b*ln(X))	LPI = sqrt(19.0809 − 2.52044*ln(DB))
	Slope	-2.52	0.18	-13.76		
GDP vs. INFR	Intercept	-15.73	5.86	-2.68	Square root-Y squared-X model: Y = (a + b*X^2)^2	GDP = (-15.73 + 15.017*INFR^2)^2
	Slope	15.01	0.68	21.98		
GDP vs. CUST	Intercept	-437.47	30.16	-14.50	Double square root model: Y = (a + b*sqrt(X))^2	GDP = (-437.47 + 333.11*sqrt(CUST))^2
	Slope	333.11	18.69	17.81		
GDP vs. ITRN	Intercept= ln(a)	5.19	0.32	16.13	Logarithmic-Y squared-X: Y = exp(a + b*X^2)	GDP = exp(5.19 + 0.40*ITRN^2)
	Slope	0.40	0.036	10.96		
GDP vs. LOGS	Intercept	-173.48	16.87	-10.28	Square root-Y logarithmic-X model: Y = (a + b*ln(X))^2	GDP = (-173.48 + 271.51*ln(LOGS))^2
	Slope	271.51	16.58	16.36		
GDP vs. TIME	Intercept	-83.41	12.63	-6.60	Square root-Y squared-X model: Y = (a + b*X^2)^2	GDP = (-83.41 + 14.99*TIME^2)^2
	Slope	14.99	1.00489	14.91		
GDP vs. TRAC	Intercept	-22807.6	2722.99	-8.37	Squared-X model: Y = a + b*X^2	GDP = -22807.6 + 4172.06*TRAC^2
	Slope	4172.06	279.54	14.92		
GDP vs. OVRL	Intercept	-244.29	19.23	-12.70	Square root-Y logarithmic-X model: Y = (a + b*ln(X))^2	GDP = (-244.29 + 327.83*ln(OVRL))^2
	Slope	327.83	18.21	17.99		

The R-Squared statistic indicates that the model as fitted explains the variability in all pairs. The correlation coefficient values indicate moderately strong relationships between the variables. The standard error of the estimate shows the standard deviation of the residuals.

The mean absolute error is the average value of the residuals. The Durbin–Watson statistic tests the residuals to determine whether there is any significant correlation based on the order in which they occur in the data. Since the p-value is greater than 0.05, there is no indication of serial autocorrelation in the residuals at the 95% confidence level (see Table 4).

Table 4. Statistics on pairs of variables

Measures	LPI vs. DB	GDP versus						
		INFR	CUST	ITRN	LOGS	TIME	TRAC	OVRL
Corr. Coeff.	-0.75	0.86	0.81	0.65	0.79	0.76	0.76	0.81
R-squared	56.48	75.24	66.62	43.04	62.75	58.32	58.34	67.06
R-squared (adjusted for d.f.)	56.18	75.08	66.41	42.68	62.52	58.06	58.08	66.85
Standard Error of Est.	2.25	36.40	42.26	1.17	44.65	47.23	13440.7	41.99
Mean absolute error	1.71	26.16	30.62	0.93	31.79	37.28	8213.86	31.01
Durbin-Watson statistic	2.14 P=0.81	1.95 P=0.39	1.97 P=0.43	2.15 P=0.84	2.004 P=0.51	1.88 P=0.23	1.90 P=0.27	2.00162 P=0.50
Lag 1 residual autocorr.	-0.08	0.02	0.01	-0.08	-0.002	0.057	0.046	-0.001

Some extreme values are found in the regression procedure. These unusual findings are depicted in Table 5a and 5b. Table 5a of unusual residuals lists all observations that have studentized residuals greater than 3 in absolute value. Table 5b of unusual residuals lists all observations that have studentized residuals less than 3 but greater than 2 in absolute value. Studentized residuals measure how many standard deviations each observed value deviates from a model fitted using all of the data except that observation.

Table 5a. Unusual residuals having studentized residuals over 3 in absolute value.

Variable (X)	Country name	X	Y (GDP)	Residual from the predicted Y	Studentized residual
INFR	Luxembourg	4.06	115038.0	61302.2	3.08
	Qatar	2.75	92501.5	82929.2	6.35
CUST	Qatar	2.25	92501.5	88632.7	6.44
ITRN	-	-	-	-	-
LOGS	Luxembourg	3.67	115038.0	82803.9	3.76
	Qatar	2.57	92501.5	85645.6	5.39
TIME	-	-	-	-	-
TRAC	Luxembourg	3.92	115038.0	73736.0	6.17
	Norway	4.1	98102.5	50777.8	4.02
	Qatar	3.09	92501.5	75473.9	6.28
OVRL	Luxembourg	3.98	115038.0	71553.4	3.25
	Qatar	2.95	92501.5	80324.0	4.96

Table 5b. Unusual residuals having studentized residuals between 2 and 3 in absolute value.

Variable (X)	Country name	X	Y (GDP)	Residual from the predicted Y	Studentized residual
INFR	The Bahamas	2.4	22431.0	5008.33	2.20
	China	3.54	5444.79	29742.8	-2.79
	India	2.91	1488.52	12418.4	-2.03
	Kuwait	3.33	62664.1	22739.3	2.81
CUST	Congo. D.R.	2.6	230.856	9931.85	-2.02
	Kuwait	3.03	62664.1	20271.1	2.61
	Luxembourg	4.04	115038.	53860.7	2.63
	Norway	3.86	98102.5	47086.2	2.35
	Uganda	2.84	487.105	15351.7	-2.46
ITRN	Botswana	1.91	8680.31	785.841	2.09
	Congo. D.R.	2.56	230.856	2541.41	-2.07
	Ethiopia	2.76	374.215	3906.09	-2.02
	Haiti	3.17	725.633	10430.1	-2.31
	Madagascar	3.06	466.663	7907.86	-2.45
	Oman	2.31	25220.6	1554.09	2.43
	Qatar	2.92	92501.5	5638.73	2.42
	Uganda	3.02	487.105	7167.9	-2.33
LOGS	China	3.49	5444.79	27517.4	-2.10
	Congo. D.R.	2.93	230.856	14017.5	-2.35
	India	3.16	1488.52	19297.0	-2.29
	Kuwait	3.11	62664.1	18112.7	2.65
	Norway	3.85	98102.5	37071.2	2.79
	Oman	2.37	25220.6	3697.01	2.23
TIME	Congo. Rep.	4.0	3562.54	24475.7	-2.08
	Iceland	3.27	44072.3	5911.44	2.89
	Kuwait	3.7	62664.1	14839.3	2.79
	Luxembourg	4.58	115038.	53384.4	2.37
	Norway	4.35	98102.5	40104.0	2.46
	Poland	4.52	13462.9	49669.0	-2.34
	Qatar	4.09	92501.5	28010.2	2.99
	Slovenia	3.1	24141.9	3678.62	2.03
	Switzerland	4.2	80390.8	32773.0	2.22
TRAC	Kuwait	3.44	62664.1	26562.8	2.75
	Oman	2.04	25220.6	-5445.19	2.33
	South Africa	3.73	8070.03	35237.8	-2.06
	Switzerland	4.27	80390.8	53261.1	2.09
OVRL	China	3.49	5444.79	27376.7	-2.23
	Eritrea	1.7	481.732	-	2.29
	India	3.12	1488.52	16568.7	-2.18
	Kuwait	3.28	62664.1	21058.2	2.56
	Namibia	2.02	5292.89	-	2.11
	Norway	3.93	98102.5	41773.2	2.68

3.2 Clustering

Clustering refers to the grouping of records, observations or cases into classes of similar objects. A cluster is a set of records that are similar to each other and dissimilar to the records in other clusters. Arrangement clustering differs in that there is no target variable for clustering (Larose 2005). The task of clustering does not seek to classify, estimate or predict the value of a target variable. Instead, clustering algorithms aim to segment the data set into relatively homogeneous subgroups or clusters, where the similarity of cases within the cluster is maximized and the resemblance to folders outside of this group is minimized (Larose 2005).

The k-means clustering algorithm is a straightforward and effective algorithm for finding clusters in data. The algorithm proceeds as follows (Larose 2005):

- Step 1: Ask the user how many k clusters the data set should be partitioned into.
- Step 2: Randomly assign k records to be the center locations of the initial cluster.
- Step 3: For each record, find the nearest cluster center. Thus, in a sense, each cluster center "owns" a subset of the records, thereby representing a partition of the data set. We therefore have k clusters, C1, C2, C3, ...,Ck.
- Step 4: For each of the k clusters, find the cluster centroid and update the location of each cluster center to the new value of the centroid.
- Step 5: Repeat steps 3 to 5 until convergence or termination.

Table 6. Summary of clustering.

Indicator	Total clusters	Cluster no:	1	2	3	4	5	6	7	8	9	10
LPI_1	7	Cases	1	3	9	52	48	40	28	-	-	-
		(%)	0.55	1.65	4.97	28.72	26.51	22.09	15.46	-	-	-
		Mean	1.17	1.66	2.01	2.42	2.77	3.31	3.98	-	-	-
LPI_2	6	Cases	3	25	48	48	24	33	-	-	-	-
		(%)	1.65	13.81	26.51	26.51	13.25	18.23	-	-	-	-
		Mean	1.47	2.08	2.35	2.67	3.15	3.81	-	-	-	-
LPI_3	4	Cases	4	52	67	58	-	-	-	-	-	-
		(%)	2.20	28.72	37.01	32.04	-	-	-	-	-	-
		Mean	1.65	2.39	2.82	3.34	3.84	-	-	-	-	-
LPI_4	10	Cases	1	1	2	5	22	39	41	25	25	20
		(%)	0.55	0.55	1.10	2.76	12.15	21.54	22.65	13.81	13.81	11.04
		Mean	1.33	1.50	1.65	1.82	2.02	2.19	2.40	2.74	3.26	3.78
LPI_5	6	Cases	1	8	30	52	49	41	-	-	-	-
		(%)	0.55	4.41	16.57	28.72	27.07	22.65	-	-	-	-
		Mean	1.38	2.35	2.83	3.16	3.60	4.16	-	-	-	-
LPI_6	7	Cases	6	17	32	41	27	26	32	-	-	-
		(%)	3.31	9.39	17.67	22.65	14.91	14.36	17.67	-	-	-
		Mean	1.54	1.82	2.06	2.34	2.61	3.09	3.88	-	-	-
LPI_7	9	Cases	1	1	6	16	26	35	39	30	27	-
		(%)	0.55	0.55	3.31	8.83	14.36	19.33	21.54	16.57	14.91	-
		Mean	1.34	1.70	2.05	2.27	2.42	2.60	2.82	3.29	3.85	-

For each of the variables (LPI_1 to LPI_7), the clustering algorithm generated clusters based on the distances calculated. Then, the algorithm placed countries into each cluster. Details of the clustering are depicted in Table 6. More details on the algorithm's placement of each country can be found in the appendix. Table 6 also shows the number of clusters for all pairs of LPIs. LPI_1 represents the efficiency of the clearance process, LPI_2 the quality of trade and transport-related infrastructure, LPI_3 the ease of organizing expeditions at competitive prices, LPI_4 the quality of logistics services, LPI_5 the ability to track and trace shipments, LPI_6 the frequency with which shipments reach the consignee within the time limit and LPI_7 overall logistics performance. The next section describes the research findings and discusses the results.

4. Findings and discussion

In Section 3, the correlations among the GDP variable and the seven logistics performance variables were investigated, with statistically significant positive correlations found among them (see Table 2). Even though the strength of these correlations varies, there exist moderately strong correlations between all the logistics performance variables and GDP.

In the next step, regression analyses were performed and the best-fitting models were explored. The relationships between each pair of logistics performance variables and GDP were then depicted (see Figure 1). Based on the best-fitted model, robust and the best-fitting mathematical equations for the relationship between each pair of variables were investigated. The best-fitted regression models are listed in Table 3. For instance, the relationship between GDP and INFR can best be described by this formula: $GDP = (-15.73 + 15.017*INFR^2)^2$ (see Table 3 for other fitting formulas). As an example, from the found formula, if a country has a GDP value of US$15,000 per capita, then it is highly likely to have a quality of trade and transport-related infrastructure score of about 3 out of 5. Indeed, the higher the GDP value of a country, the more likely it is to have higher logistics performance scores for all seven variables, and vice versa.

The R-Squared statistic is also shown in Table 4, which indicates that the model as fitted explains the variability in all pairs. In Table 5a, certain countries were found to have unusual logistics performance scores based on their GDP values, such as Luxembourg, Qatar and Norway. Based on the best-fitted regression models, these countries were expected to achieve much higher scores. For instance, Qatar has low scores for the INFR, CUST, LOGS, TRAC and OVRL variables.

Table 5b shows the unusual residuals lists of all observations that have studentized residuals less than 3 but greater than 2 in absolute value. Some countries were found to have unusual logistics performance scores based on their GDP values (excluding Norway, Luxembourg and Switzerland, as they performed well enough). Based on the estimated expectations of each individual score, as the best-fitted regression models suggest, Kuwait and the Bahamas have low scores for INFR, whereas China and India perform better. Kuwait has a low expected score for CUST, while Uganda and the Democratic Republic of Congo perform better than expected. For ITRN, Botswana, Oman and Qatar do not perform as well as expected, whereas the Democratic Republic of Congo, Ethiopia, Haiti, Madagascar and Uganda have a relatively good performance. For LOGS, Kuwait and Oman do not perform better than expected, although China, India and the Democratic Republic of Congo do. For TIME, Iceland, Kuwait, Qatar and Slovenia do not perform to expectations but the Republic of Congo and Poland do. For TRAC, Kuwait and Oman do not performance as expected, but South Africa performs well. For OVRL, China and India perform better, whereas Eritrea, Kuwait and Namibia have lower scores than those expected.

Figures 2 and 3 show the sample countries' positions based on the cluster analysis described in Section 3.2. Countries colored lighter gray indicate good performance, whereas darker gray indicates poorer performing countries. For more details on the countries/economies, refer to the appendix.

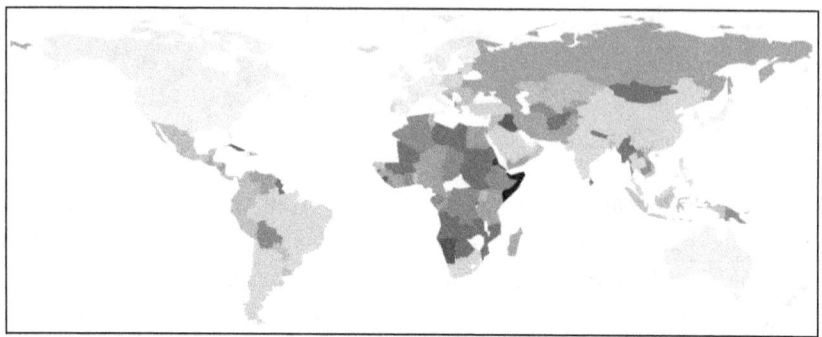

Figure 2. The overall logistics performance (LPI 7) based on clustering.

The leading LPI-ranked countries tend to be developed economies that serve as major global transport and logistics hubs (e.g. Singapore, which occupies first place) or that have a strong services industry (e.g. Switzerland). Logistics services in these countries tend to benefit from economies of scale and are often the source of innovation and technological change (Aktas *et al.* 2011). At the bottom of the rankings are low-income countries that are landlocked or geographically isolated or countries isolated because of conflict or serious governance problems, such as Afghanistan (World Bank 2008). Logistics costs account for 30% of total GDP in some developing countries, whereas this ratio is only about 10% in developed economies. This difference is clearly important for a country's competitiveness (Aktas *et al.* 2011). In fact, developing countries, particularly in Africa and Central Asia, have the most limited supply because they usually suffer from difficult geographical locations and features, poor access to logistics services in neighboring countries and high transportation costs (World Bank 2008).

Transport has been identified as one of the most important elements responsible for creating good economic conditions in a region or country (Murthy and Mohle 2001). Scholarly consensus suggests that the availability and reliability of transport links are considered by companies to be important for achieving high levels of efficiency (Cole 2005). Transport infrastructure can also play an important role in attracting investment, serving areas that are more peripheral and encouraging economic regeneration (Cole 2005). Good transportation planning, policy and programs put forward by the decision maker can thus develop a sustainable and efficient transportation system (Murthy and Mohle 2001). For example, good transit systems can shape urban development and land use measures. Another example is the development of suburbs around highways (Murthy and Mohle 2001). Therefore, mobility needs should be met by land use and a balanced efficient transportation system in order to improve the quality of life in a region or country (Murthy and Mohle 2001).

Logistics in lagging regions are the product of a complex interaction influenced by geography as well as by the decisions of many producers, consumers, transport/other service providers and governments. Logistics services in lagging regions are mainly related to supply chains in the agricultural sector (Brar *et al.* 2010). However, many of the lessons learned by rural economies are also relevant for small and medium-sized enterprises in urban areas. Strategies can be simple consolidation services provided by traders or highly developed forms of vertical integration (Brar *et al.* 2010). These could be useful in low-income countries that are developing basic commercial corridors, but which are challenged to connect the hinterland corridor regionally or globally (Brar *et al.* 2010).

The fundamental problem with logistics services in lagging regions is low demand both spatially and temporally (Brar *et al.* 2010). Special measures are therefore needed to encourage and facilitate the consolidation of volumes in order to reduce the unit costs of logistics services (Brar *et al.* 2010). Strategies encompass all the main dimensions of logistics, including the provision of adequate infrastructure, services, payment systems and coordination mechanisms between producers (Brar *et al.* 2010). The development of basic infrastructure to adjust the purpose, type and location of transport infrastructure has a great influence on logistics performance. Moreover, strategic investment in the public sector may also encourage potential buyers and sellers to engage in market production and lay the foundation for the private sector to provide logistics services (Brar *et al.* 2010). Further, inventions that bring inputs closer together, thereby reducing spatial dispersion, will tend to increase the volume of trade (Brar *et al.* 2010).

It is argued that the exporters and importers of landlocked developing countries face high logistics costs, which are detrimental to their competitiveness in global markets (Arvis *et al.* 2010). These high costs are driven by the unreliability of logistics suppliers and low predictability, which result primarily from rent-seeking and governance issues (which tend to proliferate in environments that have low volumes) (Arvis *et al.* 2010). The rapidly growing interest in trade facilitation has stimulated many initiatives and projects aimed at improving the competitiveness of firms in developing countries. As landlocked countries depend on transport corridors, foreign trade has a direct interest in facilitating trade and lowering transport costs for goods and services (Arvis *et al.* 2010). Unfortunately, initiatives in this field have not always been supported by a good analytical understanding of the impact of these transactions or generated the most value for the money allocated (Arvis *et al.* 2010).

Based on the wealth of information, data and analysis presented herein, we can conclude that in developed countries that already have a well-connected and high-quality transport infrastructure, subsequent high investment in this infrastructure will not result in further economic growth (Banister and Berechman 1999). In this regard, investment in transport infrastructure acts as a complement to other underlying conditions, which must also be satisfied if the pursuit of economic development is to take place (Banister and Berechman 1999). Therefore, additional investment in transport is not a necessary condition, but it does serve as a supporting role when other factors are at work (Banister and Berechman 1999).

The direct effects of transport infrastructure are mainly the economic consequences of the construction, maintenance and repair of infrastructure (Martin 1999). In most EU countries, the economic importance of the transport sector is considerable and these effects may become even more important at the regional level (Martin 1999). Hence, reducing transportation costs through improved transport infrastructure reduces trade barriers for many countries (Limao and Venables 2001). As discussed earlier, the cost of transportation is one of the biggest obstacles to international trade (World Bank 2012, Anderson and van Wincoop 2004). Therefore, the simple removal of barriers to international trade policy is not sufficient to achieve all the benefits of international integration law (World Bank 2012). High transport costs reduce the profit margins of domestic producers and thus their competitiveness. Therefore, reduction in transport costs leads to a more than proportional increase in international trade and substantial increases in overall income, especially in developing countries (World Bank 2012, Behar and Venables 2011, Canning and Bennathan

2007). There has long been an implicit assumption of a positive and causal link between transport and development, implying that countries, regions or cities that attract a high proportion of investment in transport have a competitive advantage over places that have been less successful in obtaining investment (Banister 1995).

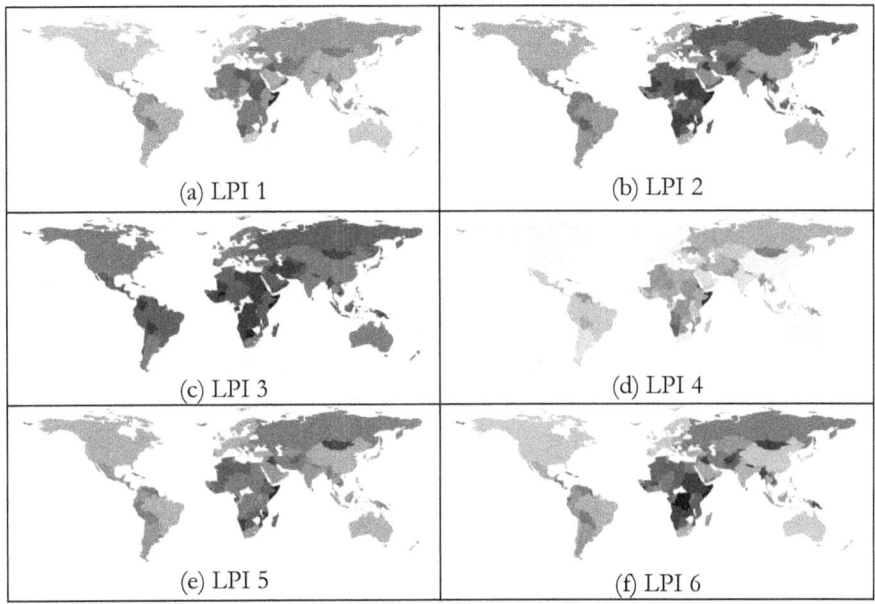

Figure 3. In each figure, countries with lighter grays indicate good performance; countries with darker grays are not good performing countries. (a) LPI 1, (b) LPI 2, (c) LPI 3, (d) LPI 4, (e) LPI 5, (f) LPI 6

Designing efficient and cost-effective energy and transportation systems that aim to improve the current environmental conditions is a major challenge. Given the world's limited natural resources and high energy demand, large-scale modeling is becoming increasingly important to understand the mechanisms that degrade energy and resources and to develop systematic approaches to improve systems and, therefore, reduce the environmental impact (Haldenbilen 2006). Another increasingly important change is the growing threat of terrorism and vulnerability owing to natural disasters and climate change (Van Geenhuizen *et al.* 2007), while policymakers are under pressure to realize concrete transport infrastructure projects and implement the necessary major changes to meet future challenges (Van Geenhuizen *et al.* 2007).

A strong economy, a sustainable environment and an inclusive society are three sustainable policies that affect the transport field. They all influence development (some require initiatives by protecting other areas of development) and movement patterns (Cole 2005). As domestic production per capita increases, so does the range of human activities, both for society as a whole and for individual lifestyles. Thus, each development proposal must be examined not only for its economic, environmental and social impacts, but also for its implications for transport. Efficient transportation is critical to the efficiency of an economy (Cole 2005). A policy of improving transport can thus unlock the economic potential unfulfilled in an area, reduce transportation costs, increase accessibility, particularly for sectors of great importance such as manufacturing, distribution and tourism, change the perception of an area and promote economic activity (Cole 2005).

Beyond these gains from cross-border trade, international market access and connectivity to global production networks attract foreign direct investment. Improvements in transport infrastructure can therefore increase the competitiveness and productivity of connected zones (World Bank 2012) as well as economic development in developing countries.

In particular, lower transportation costs boost productivity and economic growth through three mechanisms (World Bank 2012, World Development Report 2009, Coe and Helpman 1995):

(1) They enlarge the market areas of firms and reduce the unit production costs of goods and services with high fixed costs,
(2) In industries with increasing returns to scale in production, lower transport costs lead to agglomeration economies, which offer consumers more consumption variety and allow for a larger number of producers of specialized intermediate goods to localize in one city and
(3) Lower transport costs ensure access to international markets and imports of intermediate goods, which strengthen growth through international knowledge spillovers.

5. Conclusion

Seven aspects of logistics performance were examined in the present study by analyzing correlations among logistics performance indicators. The presented findings show that GDP plays an important role in determining a country's logistics performance. There is a moderately strong relationship between all logistics performance indicators and GDP. In addition, countries' DB scores are correlated with all pairs of logistics performance scores as well as with GDP. This finding implies that the lower the GDP or the DB score of a country, the more likely it is to have a low logistics performance score and vice versa.

Then, cluster analysis was performed on the logistics performance indicators to group similar countries based on the choice of clustering algorithm. This approach provided unbiased groupings of countries and allowed us to visualize countries' positioning. It was no surprise that developing and developed countries were listed in different clusters. Thus, the GDP per capita of a country allows us to predict pairs of logistics performance aspects for both developing and developed countries. Based on the presented research, it is therefore possible to predict logistics performances from GDP and DB scores.

As supply chains are so varied and complex, logistics performance depends on many factors, such as services, investment and policies. Infrastructure construction, the development of regulatory regimes for transport services and the design and implementation of efficient customs clearance procedures are all areas in which governments play an important role. Exporters and importers in developing countries face high logistics costs, which negatively affect their competitiveness in global markets. These high logistics costs are not usually the result of poor road infrastructure; rather the low reliability and predictability of logistics services tends to result in rent-seeking behavior and governance issues, which increases uncertainty throughout the supply chain. Improvements in global logistics are also being driven by innovation and increases in global trade. However, while policies and investments that strengthen logistics services contribute to the modernization of practices and to more efficient country-level performances, logistics performance in many developing countries still lags behind that in developed nations.

There is a bidirectional link between economic development and logistics performance. Therefore, it is essential for policymakers in the transport field, especially those in developing countries, to take account of various important logistics decisions. The main areas for improvement include increasing the quality of logistics services, developing and improving logistics infrastructure, promoting cooperation and coordination among logistics services providers, investing into IT, reducing logistics costs and increasing training on all aspects of supply chain management.

6. References

Aktas, E., Agaran, B., Ulengin, F., & Onsel, S. (2011). The use of outsourcing logistics activities: The case of Turkey, *Transportation Research Part C: Emerging Technologies*, 19(5), 833-852. doi: 10.1016/j.trc.2011.02.005

Arnold, J., Arvis, J. F., & Mustra, M.A. (2010). *Trade and Transport Facilitation Assessment: A Practical Toolkit to Improve the Trade Logistics and Competitiveness of Countries*, Herndon, VA, USA: World Bank Publications. p 2.

Arvis, J. F. (2007). *Connecting to compete: trade logistics in the global economy*, Washington: The World Bank. International Trade Department

Arvis, J. F., Marteau, J. F., & Raballand, G. (2010). *Directions in Development: Cost of Being Landlocked: Logistics Costs and Supply Chain Reliability*, Herndon, VA, USA: World Bank Publications. p xi-77.

Balestreri, E. J., Rutherford, T. F. & Tarr, D. G. (2009). Modeling services liberalization: the case of Kenya, *Economic Modeling*, 26(3): 668–679.

Banister, D. (1995). *Transport and Urban Development*, London, GBR: Spon Press, pp. 12-289.

Banister, D., & Berechman, J. (1999). *Transport Investment and Economic Development*, London, GBR: Routledge, p 14.

Banomyong, R., Cook, P., & Kent, P. (2008). Formulating regional logistics development policy: the case of ASEAN, *International Journal of Logistics: Research and Applications*, 5(5): 359–379.

Behar, A. & Manner, P. (2008). *Logistics and exports, African Economics Working Paper Series 293*. CSAE WPS/2008-13. Oxford: University of Oxford.

Bonacich, E., & Wilson, J. B. (2008). *Getting the Goods: Ports, Labor, and the Logistics Revolution*, Ithaca, NY, USA: Cornell University Press. p 241.

Brar, S., Farley, S.E., Hawkins, R. (2010). *Logistics in Lagging Regions: Overcoming Local Barriers to Global Connectivity*, Herndon, VA, USA: World Bank Publications. p x-67.

Canning, D., & Bennathan, E. (2007). The Rate of Return to Transportation Infrastructure, in OECD/ECMT Transport Research Center (ed.), *Transport Infrastructure Investment and Economic Productivity*, Roundtable 132, Paris.

Clark, X., Dollar, D., & Micco, A. (2004). 'Port efficiency, maritime transport cost, and bilateral trade', *Journal of Development Economics*, 75:

417–450.

Coe, D. T., & Helpman, E. (1995). International R&D Spillovers, *European Economic Review*, 39

Cole, S. (2005). *Applied Transport Economics: Policy, Management and Decision Making*, London, GBR: Kogan Page Ltd., p 429.

de Groot, H.L.F., Linders G.J., Rietveld P., & Subramanian, U. (2004). The Institutional Determinants of Bilateral Trade Patterns, *Kyklos* 57 (1): 103-24.

de Souza, R. (2007). *An investigation into the measures affecting the integration of ASEAN's priority sectors: the case of logistics*, Jakarta: ASEAN Secretariat. REPSF Project No. 06/001d, Report submitted to the ASEAN Secretariat

Decreux, I., & Fontagne, L. (2006). *A quantitative assessment of the outcome of the Doha development agenda*, CEPII Working Paper 2006–10. CEPII

Dennis, A. (2006). *The impact of regional trade agreements and trade facilitation in the Middle East and North Africa region*, World Bank Policy Research Working Paper 3837. Washington, DC: World Bank.

Dollar, D., Hallward-Driemeier, M., & Mengistae, T. (2004). *Investment Climate and International Integration*, Policy Research Working Paper 3323. World Bank, Washington, D.C.

Gallup, J., Sachs, J., & Mellinger, A. (1998). *Geography and Economic Development*, NBER Working Paper W6849, Cambridge, MA.

Gannon, C., Liu, Z. (1997). *Poverty and transport*, Washington: The World Bank. TWU Discussion Papers, TWU-30

Goldsby, T.J., & Martichenko, R. (2005). *Lean Six Sigma Logistics*. Boca Raton, FL, USA: J. Ross Publishing, Incorporated. p 30.

Haldenbilen, S. (2006). Fuel price determination in transportation sector using predicted energy and transport demand, *Energy Policy*, 34(17), 3078-3086.

Hausman, W. H., Lee, H. L., & Subramanian, U. (2013). The Impact of Logistics Performance on Trade. *Production and Operations Management*, 22(2), 236-252. doi: 10.1111/j.1937-5956.2011.01312.x

Hausman, W. H. (2004). Supply Chain Performance Metrics, *The Practice of Supply Chain Management: Where Theory and Application Converge*, 62, pp. 61-73: Springer US.

Hausmann, R. (2001). *Prisoners of Geography*, In Foreign Policy, 122 (January/February), pp. 44– 53.

Henderson, J.V., Shalizi, Z. & Venables, A.J. (2001). Geography and development, *Journal of Economic Geography*, 1: 81–106.

Hoekman, B., & Nicita, A. (2010). Assessing the Doha Round: Market access, transactions costs and aid for trade facilitation, *The Journal of International Trade & Economic Development*, 19: 65–79.

Hummels, D. (2000). *Have international transport costs declined?*, Chicago, Illinois: Purdue University. Unpublished academic work

Hummels, D. (2001). *Time as a Trade Barrier*, Working paper. Purdue University, Department of Economics, West Lafayette, Ind.

Ireland, R. K. (2004). *Supply Chain Collaboration: An Implementation Guide*, Boca Raton, FL, USA: J. Ross Publishing, Incorporated, 2004. p 8.

Iwanow, T., & Kirkpatrick, C. (2009). Trade facilitation and manufactured exports: Is Africa different?, *Word Development*, 37: 1039–1050.

Keil, R., & Young, D. (2008). Transportation: the bottleneck of regional competitiveness in Toronto. *Environment and Planning C: Government and Policy*, 26(4): 728–751.

Krugman, P. (1991). *Geography and Trade*, Leuven University Press, Belgium.

Krugman, P. (1991). Increasing returns and economic geography, *Journal of Political Economy*, 99: 483–499.

Lai, K.-H., & Cheng, T.C.E. (2009). *Just-in-Time Logistics*, Abingdon, Oxon, GBR: Ashgate Publishing Group. p xvi.

Larose, D. T. (2005). *Discovering Knowledge in Data: An Introduction to Data Mining*, Hoboken, NJ, USA: Wiley. p 147.

Lee, G. (2008). Panel Cointegration Estimation of International Knowledge Spillovers, *Global Economic Review*, 37: 1

Limao, N., & Venables, A. J. (2001). 'Infrastructure, geographical disadvantage, transport costs, and trade', *World Bank Economic Review*, 15(3), 451-479. doi: DOI 10.1093/wber/15.3.451

Lowe, D. (2002). *Dictionary of Transport and Logistics*, London, GBR: Kogan Page Ltd., 2002. p 147.

Mackellar, L., Woergoetter, A., & Woerz, J. (2000). *Economic Development Problems of Landlocked Countries*, IHS Working Paper Number 14, Vienna.

Márquez, L., Martinez-Zarzoso, I., Perez, E., & Wilmsmeier, G. (2007). Determinantes de los costes de transporte marítimos. El caso de las exportaciones españolas, *Información Comercial Española*, 834: 79–93.

Márquez-Ramos, L., Martinez-Zarzoso, I., & Suarez-Burguet, C. (2011). 'Trade policy versus trade facilitation: An application using Good Old

OLS', *Economics-The Open-Access, Open-Assessment E-Journal*, 38: 1–33.

Martin, R. (1999). '*Regional Dimension in European Public Policy: Convergence or Divergence?*', New York, NY USA: Palgrave Macmillan, p 143.

Martinez-Zarzoso, I., Perez-García, E. & Suarez-Burguet, C. (2008). 'Do transport cost have a differential effect on trade and the sectoral level', *Applied Economics*, 40: 3145–3157.

McCallum, J. (1995). 'National Borders Matter: Canada-US Regional Trade Patterns', *American Economic Review* 85: 615-23.

Moïsé, E., Orliac, T., & Minor, P. (2011). '*Trade facilitation indicators: The impact on trade costs*', OECD Trade Policy Working Papers 118. Paris: OECD Publishing.

Murthy, A.N., Mohle, H. R. (2001). '*Transportation Engineering Basics*', Reston, VA, USA: American Society of Civil Engineers, p 130.

Ng, A. K. Y., Padilha, F., & Pallis, A. A. (2012). 'Institutions, bureaucratic and logistical roles of dry ports: the Brazilian experiences', *Journal of Transport Geography*. doi: 10.1016/j.jtrangeo.2012.05.003

Nordas, H., Piermartini, R. (2004). '*Infrastructure and trade. WTO Economic Research and Statistics Division Staff*', Working Paper ERSD-2004-04. Geneva: WTO.

Norwood, J. (Editor), Casey, J. (Editor), National Research Council Staff. (2002). '*Key Transportation Indicators: Summary of a Workshop*', Washington, DC, USA: National Academies Press, p 22.

Raballand, G. (2003). '*The determinants of the negative impact of landlockedness on trade: An empirical investigation through the Central Asian case*', In Comparative Economic Studies, World Bank, Washington, D.C.

Shamim, M. (2009). '*Encyclopaedia of Logistics Management*', Volume I. Mumbai, IND: Himalaya Publishing House. p 2.

Soloaga, I., Wilson, J.S., & Mejía, A. (2006). '*Trade facilitation reform and Mexican competitiveness*', World Bank Policy Research Working Paper 3953. Washington, DC: World Bank. June

Subramanian, U., & Arnold, J. (2001). '*Forging Subregional Links in Transport and Trade Facilitation*', World Bank publication, Washington, D.C.

Subramanian, U., Anderson, W., & Lee, K. (2005). '*Measuring the Impact of the Investment Climate on Total Factor Productivity: Cases of China and Brazil*', Working paper. World Bank, Washington, D.C.

Teravaninthorn, S., Raballand, G. F. (2008). '*Transport Prices and Costs in Africa: A Review of the International Corridors*'. World Bank, Washington

D.C.
Underhill, M. D., (2010). *'Wiley Finance: Handbook of Infrastructure Investing'*, Hoboken, NJ, USA: Wiley, p 19.
Van Geenhuizen, M. (Editor), Reggiani, A. (Editor), Rietveld, P. (Editor). (2007). *'Policy Analysis of Transport Networks'*, Abingdon, Oxon, GBR: Ashgate Publishing Group, 2007. pp 16-22.
Wilmsmeier, G., Hoffmann, J., & Sanchez, R.J. (2006). 'The impact of port characteristics on international maritime transport cost', *Research in Transportation Economics*, 16: 117–140.
Wilson, J., Mann, C., & Otsuki, T. (2003). *'Trade facilitation and economic development'*, Washington, D.C: The World Bank. Policy Research Working Paper 2988
Wilson, J.S., & Otsuki, T. (2007). *'Regional integration in South Asia: What role for trade facilitation?'*, World Bank Policy Research Working Paper 4423. Washington, DC: World Bank. December
Wilson, J.S., Mann, C.L., & Otsuki, T. (2005). *'Assessing the potential benefit of trade facilitation: A global perspective'*, In Quantitative methods for assessing the effects of non-tariff measures and trade facilitation, Edited by: Dee, P. and Ferrantino, M. 121–160. Singapore: APEC Secretariat and World Scientific.
Wood, D. F., Barone, A., & Murphy, P. (2002). *'International Logistics'*, Saranac Lake, NY, USA: AMACOM Books. p 412.
World Bank. (2008). *'World Trade Indicators, 2008: Benchmarking Policy and Performance'*, Herndon, VA, USA: World Bank Publications. p 38-81.
World Bank. (2010). *'World Development Indicators'*, Herndon, VA, USA: World Bank Publications. pp 352-385.
World Bank. (2011). *'World Development Indicators: World Development Indicators 2011'*, Herndon, VA, USA: World Bank Publications. p 355.
World Bank. (2012). *'Turkey - Transport Sector Expenditure Review: Synthesis Report'*, Washington, DC. https://openknowledge.worldbank.org/handle/10986/12307 License: CC BY 3.0 Unported.
World Development Report. (2009). *'Reshaping Economic Geography'*

Part II
Global Competitiveness & Logistics Performance

Chapter 3. An empirical study on the complex relationships between logistics performances and global competitiveness

Abstract. As supply chains are complex systems with complex processes, logistics performance depends on multiple factors, such as business services, regulations, investment climate, business perceptions and policies. Organizations in the supply chain have been challenged to improve efficiency in the face of increasing complexity and global competition. It has, thus, become essential to identify relationships and to recognize relevant global competitiveness indicators that highly contribute to logistics performance. This chapter presents an empirical study on the relationship between logistics performance indicators and global competitiveness indicators and identifies the associations between them. The results indicate that some variables in global competitiveness indicators are correlated to the logistics performance indicators, whereas other variables contribute much higher to the logistics performance through canonical correlations and structural equation modeling analysis. The variables that contribute much higher others to the logistics performance are highlighted.

Keywords: logistics, supply chains, global competitiveness, canonical correlations

1. Introduction

Efficient logistics performance plays a key role in the global flow of goods and services and the ability of countries to attract and sustain investment (Hausman *et al.* 2013). The inefficiency of the logistics has been identified as a major constraint on productivity and competitiveness in developing countries carried out by previous studies on the conditions for investment facilitation and trade ("behind the border" issues) (Hausman *et al.* 2013).

When facing the challenges of global competition, companies are more focused on customer needs and on finding ways to reduce costs, improve quality and meet the growing expectations of their customers (Lai and Cheng, 2009). For this purpose, many of them found logistics as an area to include the costs and benefits of services (Lai and Cheng, 2009).

Performance measures are essential for effective management in any organization (Griffis *et al.* 2007). Performance measurement provides a necessary evaluation of services and aspects of the implementation costs of logistics in the supply chain (Griffis *et al.* 2007). Given the volume of information, logistics professionals should consider making decisions; the choice of performance measures that relate relevant and timely information is essential for effective management of logistics operations (Griffis *et al.* 2007).

Innovative measure results of strategies and action plans ensure that business systems and processes support and encourage continuous improvement (Soosay and Chapman 2006). Performance measurement identifies current or potential problems that need attention (Soosay and Chapman 2006).

Better logistics performance enables companies to move goods across borders rapidly, cheaply, and reliably (Saslavsky and Shepherd 2013). It helps to reduce overhead costs by reducing inventory levels and adopting techniques of "just-in-time" (Saslavsky and Shepherd 2013). A trade supply chain is only as strong as its weakest link (Arnold *et al.* 2010). Determining where the weakest links are and responding to targeted development interventions has become a major part of the trade facilitation agenda and logistics (Arnold *et al.* 2010). Furthermore, it is important for countries to ensure a solid performance in all areas of logistics if they want to succeed in attracting increased participation in international production networks (Saslavsky and Shepherd 2013).

This leads to a number of outstanding questions regarding the global competitiveness indicators and the logistics-performance relation. As such, what are the key logistics performance areas on which global competitiveness variables need to focus in order to increase logistics performance? Are there any correlations with global competitiveness indicators and the logistics performance indicators? How are logistics performance indicators and global competitiveness indicators canonically associated?

The remainder of this chapter is organized as follows. Section 2 reviews the literature on logistics and global competitiveness. Section 3 introduces the data and methods used for the canonical correlation analyses of the perceptions of countries' logistics efficiencies and global competitiveness variables by using various measures drawn from the World Bank and World Economic Forum (WEF)'s Global Competitiveness Index (GCI) database. It further investigates the associations between logistics performance indicators and global competitiveness indicators. Section 4 presents and discusses the empirical findings and the chapter is concluded in Section 5.

2. Literature review

Saez (2010) found that, according to some estimates, the logistics sector represents about 14 percent of global gross domestic product (GDP). In addition, logistics costs can represent 10 to 17 percent of GDP in industrialized countries (Saez 2010). The logistics sector has increased by about 10 percent per year since the early 1990s (Saez 2010), with the fastest growth rates and 3PL Logistics Services Part IV (companies that coordinate activities between 3PL) followed by the international container shipping and airfreight (Saez 2010). Research shows that by improving logistics performance in low-income countries the average middle income can boost trade by 15 percent or more (Fardoust *et al.* 2010).

Cecere and Chase (2013) indicated that the management of the supply chain is a complex system with processes of increasing complexity. They recognized that today, complexity reigns and it is a time of increasing volatility, product customization, and the proliferation of new channels

(Cecere and Chase 2013).

According to Sehgal (2011), while today's supply chains extend across most of the activities of the company chain originally described by Porter value, they are essentially a set of capabilities that organizations built to operate, survive and grow.

As recognized by Sherman (2012), facing unprecedented global competition and economic volatility, companies must turn their attention to strategic advantage and the value locked in the traditional management of the supply chain. Transforming the management of the supply chain on a journey to improve the continuous operation of the performance of excellence is no longer an option; it is a strategic mandate (Sherman 2012).

The evolution of the management of the supply chain (SCM) increased from disparate functions of logistics, transport, purchase and physical distribution to focus on integration, collaboration, visibility, reliability, flexibility and responsiveness (Sabri and Shaikh 2010). The evolution of SCM was like a vertical integration spectrum on one side and a horizontal integration with other various permutations and combinations of the two as different colors of the spectrum (Sabri and Shaikh 2010) on the other side. Companies have generally pursued one of three types SCM integration: vertical integration, lateral integration, and for some a hybrid of vertical and lateral integration (Sabri and Shaikh 2010).

There is also evidence that economic, political and social developments over the last decade appear to increase the likelihood that disturbances occur as supply chains become more complex (Khan and Zsidisin 2011).

Khan and Zsidisin (2011) stated that even in the supply chains established, issues such as terrorism, epidemics and natural disasters, all have the power to disrupt supply chains. In addition, they recognized that we live in an era of rapidly changing technology, rapid progress in product markets and customer expectations for better products, lower prices and faster response time. Add them together and you can see why the potential risks facing supply chains have increased exponentially (Khan and Zsidisin 2011).

Levesque (2011) stated that as models of the supply chain become more dynamic and complex, the demand for qualified talent supply will continue to increase. Competent leadership will be critical for the recruitment, retention and career development of logistics experts worldwide (Levesque 2011). The talented recruits expect the vision of society to be well defined, and effectively deployed (Levesque 2011), while at the same time transformational leaders understand that their job is to grow more leaders, not create more followers (Levesque 2011).

Turner (2011) noted that before a company starts doing business with a company in another country, there are many things they should know, understand and take into account. Doing business internationally is easier than it used to be; however some of the same pitfalls and obstacles still exist (Turner 2011). Two things that make international trade easier are the Internet and the fact that many companies have set up operations in different countries (Turner 2011).

Saez (2010) pointed out that the design and implementation of services trade and investment policies have become major issues for many governments in developing countries. Many services are essential inputs to production (Saez 2010). Saez (2010) also stated that the effectiveness of the services sectors is an important determinant of productivity in other sectors, whether in manufacturing or agriculture, as well as other services. Reforms that result in higher quality, lower prices and a wider variety of services are able to generate welfare gains (Saez 2010).

Haddad and Shepherd (2011) noted that, in the future, the ones who may export growth and diversifications in developing countries are developing countries themselves, as these countries play a vital role through trade. GDP growth in developing countries with low and middle-income resulted in an increase in import demand, which has played an important role in stimulating exports and promoting export diversification in low-income countries.

Blanchard (2010) stated that most of the multinational companies that provide manufacturing activity in China prefer to use global logistics providers established for imports and exports, mainly because they can reduce costs by taking advantage of global contracts and service level commitments (Blanchard 2010).

Dadush and Shaw (2011) found that even in the largest developing countries, the national economy is dwarfed by the size of the global market and sophistication. In recent years, developing countries have increased dramatically in importance as both importers and exporters, and in most cases, trade is essential to their economic success (Dadush and Shaw 2011). Indeed, if the rapid export growth does not always guarantee success, no country has sustained growth without increasing exports (Dadush and Shaw2011). In this sense, while the growth conditions must be put in place at home, it is often on the stage of world trade (measured by the increase in exports and imports) where the development succeeds or fails (Dadush and Shaw2011).

McLinden *et al.* (2010) noted that a clearance process that is obsolete and overly bureaucratic imposed by customs and other agencies is now considered to be much more important for trade than tariffs are as obstacles. Systems, cumbersome procedures and inadequate infrastructure all increase transaction costs and extend the deadlines for clearance of imports, exports and goods in transit (McLinden *et al.* 2010).

For the past decade, global competition has become an important force for almost all businesses, regardless of their location (Sledge 2011). Even domestic companies should consider all countries as rivals and the business world to be in constant evolution (Sledge 2011). Global competition is a concept that has attracted the attention of employers, officers, government officials and researchers (Sledge 2011).

National competitiveness is a complex and dynamic concept that transcends macro foundations - and the creation of micro-economic prosperity and value (Moses 2010). This is not just about economics, law and business, but also draws on the wider social, political, cultural, geographical and historical institutional arrangements, resources, values and practices of a country (Moses 2010).

Today the world is more complex, interdependent and interconnected than in any other time in human history. Increasingly, we are faced with the challenges of adaptation and opportunities for deep processing (Koenitzer 2013). This new leadership context requires organizations to manage the strategic agility of success and improve the resilience of risks (Koenitzer 2013). More broadly, we must strengthen the elastic energy in all sectors of society, especially in the financial services industry (Koenitzer 2013).

Studies of logistics, business and transport in relation to the performance have been made by many authors. Current research reflects the increasing amount of international literature in this area based on different viewpoints. For example, the factors that explain the logistics performance at country level were analyzed by Gogoneata (2008), while trade policy, trade costs and trade countries were examined by Hoekman and Nicita (2011). In addition, the impact of trade logistics performance on trade has been studied by Hausman *et al.* (2013).

Similarly, the performance of logistics within the supply chain was studied by Green *et al.* (2008), while Liu *et al.* (2011) studied the performance of 3PL and services. The relationship between performance and the provision of logistics services was assessed by Liu and Lyon (2011), the integration of relations in the supply chain between the product / process strategy and service performance has been studied by Droge *et al.* (2012), the efficiency, effectiveness and differentiation of logistics performance has been central to Fugate *et al.* (2010) and Grawe *et al.* (2011) offers a synthesis of knowledge and innovation to increase flexibility and operational performance in the logistics processes.

On a sectoral basis Garcia *et al.* (2012) developed a framework for measuring the performance of logistics in the wine industry, while a similar study in the automotive industry was conducted by Schmitz and Platts (2004). In addition, another study evaluated the distribution of pharmaceuticals and discussed how to combine business performance and logistics individually (Spindler 2010).

The present study adds another dimension to the existing literature. In this regard, by using statistical methods, this study contributes by providing a better understanding to policymakers. Specifically, it differs from previous works in that it investigates statistically significant relationships for logistics performance.

3. Data and methods

In this study, two main types of data sources are used, all of which are drawn from the World Bank and WEF database. The first data set is about the perceptions of countries' logistics efficiencies and the second about global competitiveness indicators.

The World Economic Forum uses the growth competitiveness index (GCI) to measure and compare global competitiveness among the world's trading economies on an annual basis. The GCI summarizes a country's set of institutions, policies and structures, which drive its growth on the medium and long term. The WEF's GCI (2013-2014) measures national competitiveness using a complex methodology involving raw data and executive opinions. The index rests on 12 pillars categorized in three groups. These groups are "Basic requirements" (four pillars), "Efficiency enhancers" (six pillars) and "Innovation and Sophistication factors" (two pillars). Countries are rated on a seven-point scale, where a higher score indicates more competitiveness. In the "Basic requirements" group the four pillars are: institutions (1), infrastructure (2), macroeconomic stability (3), and health and primary education (4). The group "Efficiency enhancers" (with six pillars) consists of higher education and training (5), goods market efficiency (6), labor market efficiency (7), financial market sophistication (8), technological readiness (9), and market size (10). In "Innovation and Sophistication" the two pillars are: business sophistication (11) and innovation (12).

The Logistics Performance Index (LPI) of the World Bank, which measures six aspects of the environment of logistics including transportation services, identifies areas where improvements are most needed (Handjiski and Sestovic 2011). The LPI is based on a global survey of freight forwarders and express carriers and quantitative data on the performance of the logistics chain (Handjiski and Sestovic 2011). The LPI is a research initiative launched by a transport and trade facilitation alliance of several public and private organizations, conducted by the World Bank (Lopez and Shankar 2011). It evaluates the performance of logistics on six environmental aspects of logistics based on more than 5,000 country assessments by nearly 1,000 international freight forwarders (World Bank 2011). Respondents evaluate eight markets on six core dimensions on a scale from 1 (worst) to 5 (excellent) (World Bank 2011). The markets are chosen based on the largest exporting and importing countries respondent markets, random selection, and, for landlocked countries, neighboring countries that connect them with international markets (World Bank 2011).

The composite LPI summarizes areas of performance. In brief, these variables are: CUST, which stands for customs clearance process; INFR, which is the quality of trade and transport-related infrastructure; ITRN, which is the ease of arranging competitively priced shipments; LOGS, which is the quality of logistics services; TRAC, which is the ability to track and trace consignments; TIME, which is the frequency with which shipments reach the consignee within the scheduled time and OVRL, which is the overall logistics performance.

LPI variables (CUST, INFR, ITRN, LOGS, TRAC, TIME) introduce a multicollinearity issue, which poses a problem in statistical analysis. Multicollinearity occurs when the predictors included in the linear model are highly correlated (Yan 2009). In order to overcome this problem, by using the factor analysis technique, six LPI variables are factor analyzed and six components are extracted, each representing their respective variables, though factor analysis is mainly used for obtaining a small number of factors that account for most of the variability. In this exceptional case, six factors were extracted out of six variables. Together, they accounted for 100% of the variability in the original LPI data. Finally, these extracted factors are stored as *Anderson–Rubin factor scores*, which are scores uncorrelated with other factors. The multicollinearity issue for the twelve GCI variables is also solved by using the same technique. The factor loadings of the equamax rotation indicated (For more details see Tables A4 through A9, in the Appendix section).

3.1 Canonical correlation analysis of LPI and GCI scores

A generalization of principal component analysis (PCA) developed by Hotelling (1936), is canonical correlation analysis (CCA) (Timm 2002). Canonical correlation analysis is concerned with the amount of relationship (linear) between two sets of variables (Rencher 2012). The method was developed to study the relationship between two sets of variables with one or more sets of variables (Timm 2002). Canonical correlation analysis is probably the method of analysis based on the largest number of matrix algebra tools, including elements such as the Cholesky decomposition, matrix inversion, eigenvalues and eigenvectors and decomposition singular values (Brown *et al.* 2011).

This procedure finds the linear combinations of two sets of variables (LPI and GCI), which have the highest correlation between them.

Four multivariate statistics were calculated to test the null hypotheses that the canonical correlations are zero and that there is no linear relationship between the GCI and LPI variables. Since p values are less than 0.05 in the Pillais (the Pillai's trace), Hotellings (the Hotelling-Lawley trace) and Wilks (the Wilks' lambda) tests, the null hypothesis is rejected. Therefore, the alternative hypothesis that there is a linear relationship between the GCI and LPI variables is accepted. The Roy's (the Roy's greatest root) test behaves differently from the other three tests. In cases where the remaining three are not statistically significant and Roy's is statistically significant, the effect is considered not to be statistically significant (See Table 1).

Table 1. Analysis of variance. "Effect .. Within" Cells Regression. Multivariate Tests of Significance (S = 6, M = 2 1/2, N = 55)

Test Name	Value	Approx. F	Hypoth. DF	Error DF	Sig. of F
Pillais	1.45	3.09	72	702.00	0.00
Hotellings	7.41	11.36	72	662.00	0.00
Wilks	0.07	5.43	72	615.15	0.00
Roys	0.87	-	-	-	-

Table 2 presents the column root no, which is the rank of the eigenvalue data in the order, based on the eigenvalue from largest to smallest. There are as many roots as there were variables in the smaller of the two variable sets (GCI and LPI). The set of GCI variables contains twelve variables and the set of LPI variables contains six variables. Thus, the smaller set of variables contains six analysis variables and generates six roots. The relative size of the eigenvalues reflects the amount of variance in the canonical variables that can be explained by the corresponding canonical correlation. Thus, the eigenvalue corresponding to the first correlation is the largest, and all the following eigenvalues are smaller (See Table 2).

Table 2. Eigenvalues and Canonical Correlations. Significant rows are highlighted.

Root No.	Eigenvalue	%	Cumulative %	Canonical Correlation - R	R^2
1	6.71	90.56	90.56	0.93	0.87
2	0.35	4.68	95.24	0.51	0.26
3	0.15	2.00	97.24	0.36	0.13
4	0.12	1.58	98.81	0.32	0.10
5	0.06	0.76	99.57	0.23	0.05
6	0.03	0.43	100.00	0.18	0.03

Table 3 depicts the set of roots included in the null hypothesis being tested. The null hypothesis is that all correlations associated with roots in the given set are zero in the population. By testing different sets of these roots, we determine the number of dimensions required to describe the relationship between two variable groups. In this case, six sets of linear combinations have been formed. However, only two sets of linear combinations are statistically significant $p<0.05$ (See Table 3 and Figure 1).

Table 3. Dimension Reduction Analysis. Rows having $p<0.05$ are highlighted.

Roots	Wilks L.	F	Hypoth. DF	Error DF	Sig. of F
1 to 6	0.07	5.43	72	615.15	0.00
2 to 6	0.53	1.40	55	526.64	0.04
3 to 6	0.72	1.00	40	434.13	0.47
4 to 6	0.82	0.87	27	336.50	0.66
5 to 6	0.92	0.64	16	232.00	0.85
6 to 6	0.97	0.53	7	117.00	0.81

The canonical analysis summary is that the canonical R equals to 0.93, Chi^2 (72) equals to 319.6846, and p equals to 0.00.

In this case, six sets of linear combinations have been formed. However, only two sets of linear combinations are statistically significant $p<0.05$ (See table 3 and figure 1). The first set forms the strongest correlations and R^2 equals to 0.87. The first set of linear combinations with the highlighted highly contributing variables is

U_1 = $-$ 0.29×F_1 $-$ **0.35×F_2** $-$ 0.08×F_3 $-$ 0.19×F_4 $-$ 0.25×F_5 $-$ 0.23×F_6 $-$ 0.11×F_7 $-$ 0.21×F_8 $-$ **0.42×F_9** $-$ **0.41×F_10** $-$ 0.31×F_11 $-$ 0.30×F_12

and

L_1 = $-$ 0.36×F_TIME $-$ 0.36×F_ITRN $-$ 0.40×F_CUST $-$ **0.47×F_INFR** $-$ **0.45×F_TRAC** $-$ 0.37×F_LOGS

In addition, the second set of linear combinations, which is the next correlation and is substantially less strong (R^2 equals to 0.26) amongst all combinations that are uncorrelated with the first set (See table 3 and figure 1b), with the highlighted highly contributing variables is,

$U_2 = -\mathbf{0.38 \times F\_1} + 0.01 \times F\_2 - 0.28 \times F\_3 - \mathbf{0.56 \times F\_4} + 0.03 \times F\_5 + 0.10 \times F\_6 - \mathbf{0.35 \times F\_7} - 0.11 \times F\_8 + 0.04 \times F\_9 + \mathbf{0.63 \times F\_10} - 0.01 \times F\_11 + 0.01 \times F\_12$

and

$L_2 = -0.05 \times F\_TIME + \mathbf{0.37 \times F\_ITRN} - \mathbf{0.76 \times F\_CUST} + 0.29 \times F\_INFR - 0.24 \times F\_TRAC + \mathbf{0.43 \times F\_LOGS}$

where the variables have first been standardized by subtracting their means and dividing by their standard deviations. Table 3 shows the estimated correlation between each set of canonical variables. Since two of the p values are less than 0.05, those sets have statistically significant correlations at the 95% confidence level.

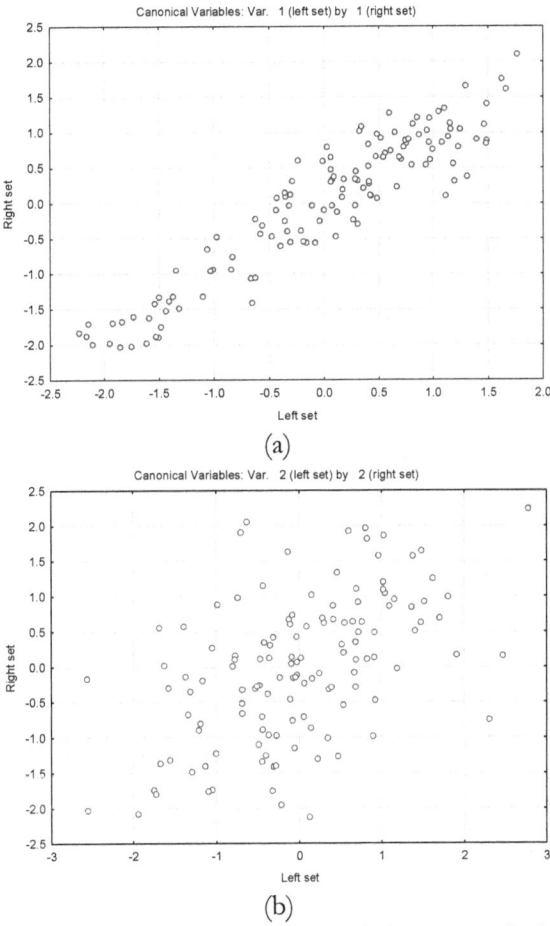

Figure 1. GCI (right set root 1) versus LPI (left set root 1), (b) GCI (right set root 2) versus LPI (left set root 2)

3.2 Structural equation modeling

Structural equation modeling (SEM) is a sophisticated and complex statistical procedure that can be used to perform both a confirmatory factor and a path analysis of quantitative variables (Cramer and Howitt 2004). It allows the determination of the statistical fit of the models showing the relationship between the variables (Howitt and Cramer 2004). Structural equation modeling allows us to look with more complexity than traditional modeling techniques or more levels (Muijs 2004) models. Rather than simply assuming that all individual variables directly affect the outcome variable, we can model the indirect effects as well (Muijs 2004). The structural equation modeling also allows us to distinguish between the manifest variables (variables that we actually measured) and the latent variables (the concepts that we are trying to measure and that the manifest variables are indicators of) (Muijs 2004).

In this section, two SEM analyses were carried out to keep one-dimensionality, which is essential for retrieving healthy results. The first analysis investigates the relationships between pillars 1 through 9 and logistics performance variables. The second analysis investigates the relationships between pillars 11 and 12 and logistics performance variables. Pillar 10 is excluded from analyses as it disturbs the overall fit.

Maximum Likelihood (ML) estimation is used for both analyses, which is suitable for low sample sizes. Chi-Square p-level are <0.05, therefore SEM models are acceptable. In addition, other statistics such as *Max. Abs. Gradient*, *ICSF Criterion* and *ICS Criterion* are close to zero, which implies that models are appropriate for analysis (See Table 4). For more details, see Appendix section, Table A10 through A19.

The significant relationships between the pillars of global competitiveness index and logistics performance are shown in Figure 2 and Table 5.

Table 4. Statistics of SEM analysis for pillars 1-9 and pillars 11-12 versus LPI

Pillars 1-9 versus LPI	
Method of Estimation: ML	Chi-Square Statistic: 39.0408
Discrepancy Function: 0.303	Degrees of Freedom: 43
Maximum Residual Cosine: 0.183	Chi-Square p-level: 0.643659
Max. Abs. Gradient: 0.0705	Steiger-Lind RMSEA
ICSF Criterion: 0.216	--->Point Estimate: 0
ICS Criterion: 0.124	-->Lower 90% Bound: 0
Boundary Conditions: 8	-->Upper 90% Bound: 0
	RMS Stand. Residual: 0.0401
Pillars 11-12 versus LPI	
Method of Estimation: ML	Chi-Square Statistic: 6.13436
Discrepancy Function: 0.0476	Degrees of Freedom: 14
Maximum Residual Cosine: 3.07E-006	Chi-Square p-value: 0.962990
Max. Abs. Gradient: 0.00954	Steiger-Lind RMSEA
ICSF Criterion: 4.11E-009	--->Point Estimate: 0
ICS Criterion: 4.57E-007	-->Lower 90% Bound: 0
Boundary Conditions: 2	-->Upper 90% Bound: 0
	RMS Stand. Residual: 0.0351

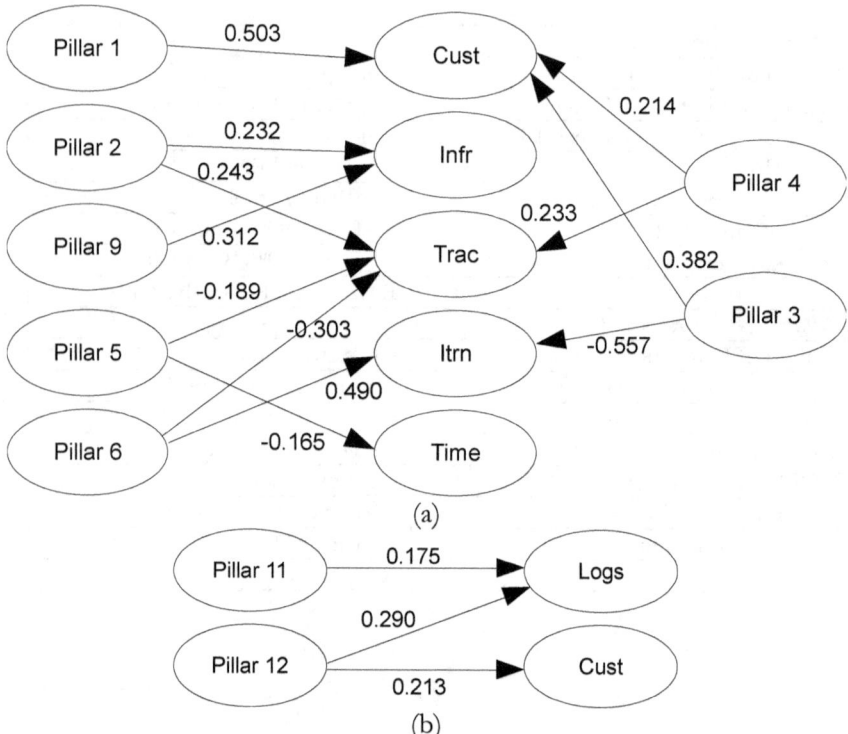

Figure 2. Significant relationships between LPI variables and GCI variables. (a) Pillars 1-9, (b) Pillars 11-12

Table 5. Significant relationships of SEM analysis

Indicator	Parameter – Estimate	Standard – Error	T – Statistic	Prob. – Level
Pillars 1-9 versus LPI				
Pillar1 → Cust	0.503	0.143	3.524	0.000
Pillar2 → Infr	0.232	0.077	2.997	0.003
Pillar2 → Trac	0.243	0.082	2.969	0.003
Pillar3 → Itrn	-0.557	0.22	-2.532	0.011
Pillar3 → Cust	0.382	0.156	2.453	0.014
Pillar4 → Cust	0.214	0.083	2.568	0.010
Pillar4 → Trac	0.233	0.082	2.851	0.004
Pillar5 → Time	-0.165	0.081	-2.028	0.043
Pillar5 → Trac	-0.189	0.081	-2.331	0.020
Pillar6 → Itrn	0.490	0.25	1.960	0.050
Pillar6 → Trac	-0.303	0.151	-2.014	0.044
Pillar9 → Infr	0.312	0.101	3.102	0.002
Pillars 11-12 versus LPI				
Pillar11 → Logs	0.175	0.083	2.103	0.035
Pillar12 → Cust	0.213	0.088	2.432	0.015
Pillar12 → Logs	0.29	0.085	3.423	0.001

4. Research findings and discussions

The first canonical correlation, U_1 and L_1, is strong with a magnitude of 0.93 and statistically significant with p<0.05 (See Table 3 and Figure 1a). There is a primarily relationship between the logistics performance variable of INFR, TRAC and the global competitiveness variable of F_9 with some contribution of F_10 and F_2. This implies that *the quality of trade and transport-related infrastructure* and *the ability to track and trace consignments* are related to the global competitiveness variables of *the technological readiness*, with some contribution of *the market size* and *infrastructure*.

The second canonical correlation, U_2 and L_2, is substantially less strong with a magnitude of 0.51 and statistically significant with p<0.05 (See Table 3 and Figure 1b). There is a relationship between the logistics performance variables of CUST, LOGS, ITRN and the global competitiveness variable of F_10 with some contribution of F_4 and F_1. The implication is that *the customs clearance process, the quality of logistics services and the ease of arranging competitively priced shipments* are related to the global competitiveness variable of *the market size* with some contribution of *the health and primary education* and *infrastructure.*

Figure 2 shows the relationships between the global competitiveness index and the logistics performance variables. Figures show that some pillars are significantly related to some of the logistics performance variables. The global competitiveness pillars, such as pillars 2 (Infrastructure), 4 (Health and Primary education), 5 (Higher education and training) and 6 (Goods market efficiency) significantly affect TRAC, which implies that the higher the score of these pillars, the higher the score in the ability to track and trace consignments (TRAC). For more details on the other relationships, see Figure 2, which is self-explanatory.

The logistics performance has recently been given attention in the context of benchmarking initiatives globally to assess the ease of doing business in different countries, and the efficiency of logistics and transport services is more increasingly seen as a major contributor to high import costs and long delays (Raballand *et al.* 2012).

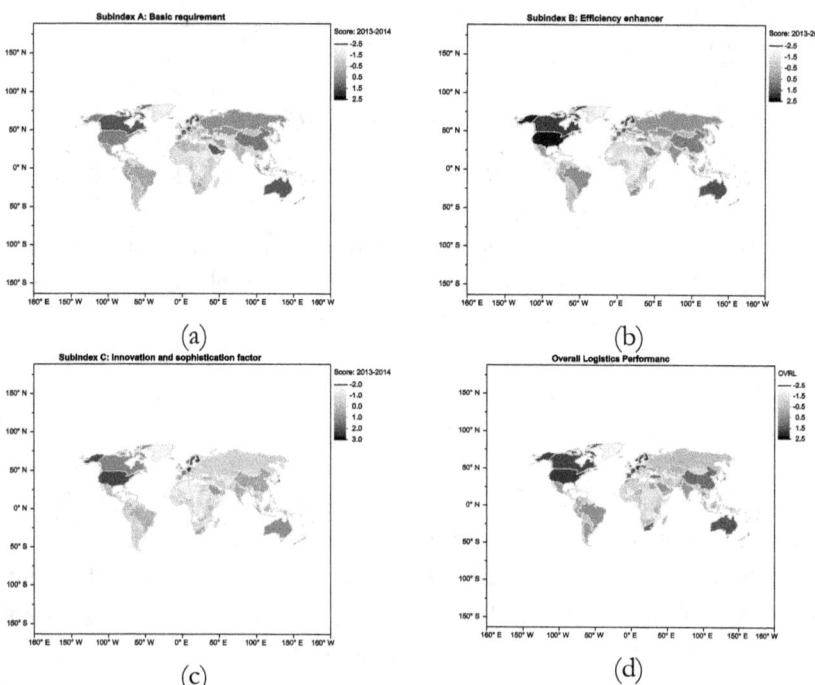

Figure 2. In each figure, countries with darker grays indicate good performance; countries with lighter grays are not well performing countries.

White regions/countries indicate unavailable data. (a) Sub-index A: Basic requirements scores, (b) Sub-index B: Efficiency enhancers scores, (c) Sub-index C: Innovation and sophistication factors scores, (d) the overall logistics performance (OVRL)

Unlike financial services, distribution, communication and professional services logistics services are a set of service industries (Saez 2010) subject to regulation to different service activities (Saez 2010). In addition, the regulation of logistics services based services means that the optimal regulatory system is difficult to develop (Saez 2010).

Companies that have an excellent logistics competence can gain a competitive advantage by providing customers with quality service (Muthiah 2010). With a performance above the industry average in terms of availability of stocks and speed and consistency of delivery, logistics companies are interesting suppliers and business partners (Muthiah 2010). The overall effect is that the goal of logistics is to achieve a level of service to the target audience at the lowest possible total cost (Muthiah 2010).

Policy makers in developing countries should continue to look for innovative ways to increase economic growth, including exports (World Bank 2008). The challenges they face are enormous, particularly because of global competition increase and taking on new forms, driven by rapid technological change and the growth of global production networks, the skills and sophisticated capabilities of which are required for level entry (World Bank 2008).

5. Conclusion

In this chapter, an empirical study on the relationship between indicators of logistics performance and GCI variables was performed. The associations between indicators of logistics performance and GCI scores were identified and the results indicate that certain variables in the GCI data are correlated with indicators of logistics performance. The significant relationships and those variables that have high contributions are highlighted.

As evidenced by the analysis, certain variables in GCI indicators contribute much more to logistics performance than other variables. In this regard, it is essential for policymakers in the logistics field to take account of those variables that have higher contributions in canonical correlations. By taking into consideration the GCI indicators, the main areas for improvement of the logistics performance include focusing more on the highlighted indicators in this study to significantly improve outcomes.

Logistics performance depends on many factors, as supply chains are complex systems with complex processes, such as business services, regulations, investment climate, perceptions of enterprises and policy. Supply chain organizations are challenged to improve efficiency in the face of increasing complexity and global competition. It became necessary to determine the relationship and recognize the relevant indicators that contribute to high logistics performance. This chapter presented an empirical study on the relationship between indicators of logistics performance and global competitiveness indicators and defined the association between the indicators of logistics performance and those of global competitiveness. The results show that some variables in the global competitiveness indicators data are correlated with the efficiency of logistics and that some variables in the global competitiveness indicators data contribute much higher to logistics performance than other variables via the canonical correlation analysis. The variables that contribute significantly higher than other variables in logistic performances have been highlighted.

6. References

Arnold, J., Arvis, J.F., Mustra, M.A. (2010). *Trade and Transport Facilitation Assessment: A Practical Toolkit to Improve the Trade Logistics and Competitiveness of Countries.* Herndon, VA, USA: World Bank Publications, p 1.

Blanchard, D. (2010). *Supply Chain Management Best Practices (2nd Edition).* Hoboken, NJ, USA: Wiley, 2010. p 127.

Brown, B. L., Hendrix, S. B., Hedges, D. W. (2011). *Multivariate Analysis for the Biobehavioral and Social Sciences: A Graphical Approach.* Hoboken, NJ, USA: Wiley. p 297-328.

Cecere, L.M., Chase, C.W. (2013). *Wiley and SAS Business Series: Bricks Matter: The Role of Supply Chains in Building Market-Driven Differentiation.* Somerset, NJ, USA: Wiley, p 151-182.

Cramer, D., Howitt, D. L. (2004). *SAGE Dictionary of Statistics: A Practical Resource for Students in the Social Sciences.* London, GBR: SAGE Publications Inc. (US), 2004. p 163.

Dadush, U., Shaw, W.J. (2011). *How Emerging Powers are Reshaping Globalization.* Washington, DC, USA: Carnegie Endowment for International Peace, p 6.

Droge, C., Vickery, S. K., and Jacobs, M. A. (2012). Does supply chain integration mediate the relationships between product/process strategy and service performance? An empirical study. *International Journal of Production Economics*, 137(2), 250-262. doi: 10.1016/j.ijpe.2012.02.005

Fardoust, S. (Editor), Kim, Y. (Editor), Sepulveda, C.P. (Editor). (2010). *Postcrisis Growth and Development: A Development Agenda for the G-20.* Herndon, VA, USA: World Bank Publications, p 148.

Fugate, B. S., Mentzer, J. T., Stank, T. P. (2010). Logistics Performance: Efficiency, Effectiveness, and Differentiation. *Journal of Business Logistics*, 31(1), 43-+.

Garcia, F. A., Marchetta, M. G., Camargo, M., Morel, L., and Forradellas, R. Q. (2012). A framework for measuring logistics performance in the wine industry. *International Journal of Production Economics*, 135(1), 284-298. doi: 10.1016/j.ijpe.2011.08.003

Gogoneata, B. (2008). An analysis of explanatory factors of logistics performance of a country. *Amfiteatru Economic*, 10(24), 143-156.

Grawe, S. J., Daugherty, P. J., and Roath, A. S. (2011). Knowledge Synthesis and Innovative Logistics Processes: Enhancing Operational Flexibility and Performance. *Journal of Business Logistics*, 32(1), 69-80.

Green, K. W., Whitten, D., Inman, R. A. (2008). The impact of logistics performance on organizational performance in a supply chain context. *Supply Chain Management-An International Journal*, 13(4), 317-327. doi: 10.1108/13598540810882206

Griffis, S. E., Goldsby, T. J., Cooper, M., Closs, D. J. (2007). Aligning Logistics Performance Measures to the Information Needs of the Firm. *Journal of Business Logistics*, 28(2), 35-56. doi: 10.1002/j.2158-1592.2007.tb00057.x

Haddad, M. (Editor), Shepherd, B. (Editor). (2011). *Managing Openness: Trade and Outward-Oriented Growth after the Crisis*. Herndon, VA, USA: World Bank Publications, p 1.

Handjiski, B., Sestovic, L. (2011). *World Bank Studies: Barriers to Trade in Services in the CEFTA Region*. Herndon, VA, USA: World Bank Publications, p 26.

Hausman, W. H., Lee, H. L., & Subramanian, U. (2013). The Impact of Logistics Performance on Trade. *Production and Operations Management*, 22(2), 236-252. doi: 10.1111/j.1937-5956.2011.01312.x

Hoekman, B., Nicita, A. (2010). Assessing the Doha Round: Market access, transactions costs and aid for trade facilitation, *The Journal of International Trade & Economic Development*, 19: 65–79.

Hotelling, H. (1936). Relations between two sets of variates. *Biometrika*, 28, 321– 377.

Khan, O. (Editor), Zsidisin, G. A. (Editor). (2011). *Handbook for Supply Chain Risk Management*. Ft. Lauderdale, FL, USA: J. Ross Publishing Inc., p 30-74.

Koenitzer, M. (2013). The World Economic Forum: A multistakeholder platform for engaging the financial services industry and its role during the global economic crisis. *Journal of Risk Management in Financial Institutions*, 6(2), 181-184.

Lai, Kee-hung, Cheng, T.C.E. (2009). *Just-in-Time Logistics*. Abingdon, Oxon, GBR: Ashgate Publishing Group, p 1.

Levesque, P. J. (2011). *Shipping Point: The Rise of China and the Future of Retail Supply Chain Management*. Hoboken NJ, USA: Wiley, p 16-278.

Liu, C. L., & Lyons, A. C. (2011). An analysis of third-party logistics performance and service provision. *Transportation Research Part E-*

Logistics and Transportation Review, 47(4), 547-570. doi: 10.1016/j.tre.2010.11.012

Liu, J. J., So, S. C. K., Choy, K. L., Lau, H., and Kwok, S. K. (2008). Performance improvement of third-party logistics providers - An integrated approach with a logistics information system. *International Journal of Technology Management*, 42(3), 226-249. doi: 10.1504/ijtm.2008.018105

Liu, W. H., Xu, X. C., Ren, Z. X., and Peng, Y. (2011). An emergency order allocation model based on multi-provider in two-echelon logistics service supply chain. *Supply Chain Management-An International Journal*, 16(6), 391-400. doi: 10.1108/13598541111171101

Lopez, J. H. (Editor), Shankar, R. (Editor). (2011). *Directions in Development: Getting the Most Out of Free Trade Agreements in Central America*. Herndon, VA, USA: World Bank Publications, 2011. p 186.

McLinden, G. (Editor), Fanta, E. (Editor), Widdowson, D. (Editor). (2010). *Border Management Modernization*. Herndon, VA, USA: World Bank Publications, p 1.

Moses, N. Kiggundu, Aareni Uruthirapathy, (2010). Canada's global and business competitiveness: competition policy reform in a changing world, *Competitiveness Review*, Vol. 20 Iss: 4, pp.288 – 304

Muijs, D. (2004). *Doing Quantitative Research in Education with SPSS*. London, GBR: SAGE Publications Inc. (US), 2004. p 217.

Muthiah, K. V. (2010). *Logistics Management and World Seaborne Trade*. Mumbai, IND: Global Media, 2010. p 1-2.

Raballand, G., Refas, S., Beuran, M. (2012). *Directions in Development: Why Does Cargo Spend Weeks in Sub-Saharan African Ports?: Lessons from Six Countries*. Herndon, VA, USA: World Bank Publications, p 18.

Rencher, A. C. (2012). *Wiley Series in Probability and Statistics: Methods of Multivariate Analysis (3rd Edition)*. Somerset, NJ, USA: Wiley. p 413.

Sabri, E, Shaikh, S. N. (2010). *Lean and Agile Value Chain Management: A Guide to the Next Level of Improvement*. Ft. Lauderdale, FL, USA: J. Ross Publishing Inc., p xi-151.

Saslavsky, D., & Shepherd, B. (2013). Facilitating international production networks: The role of trade logistics. *The Journal of International Trade & Economic Development*, 1-21. doi: 10.1080/09638199.2013.811534

Schmitz, J., & Platts, K. W. (2004). Supplier logistics performance measurement: Indications from a study in the automotive industry.

International Journal of Production Economics, 89(2), 231-243. doi: 10.1016/s0925-5273(02)00469-3

Sehgal, V. (2011). *Supply Chain as Strategic Asset: The Key to Reaching Business Goals*. Hoboken, NJ, USA: Wiley, p xxi.

Sherman, R. (2012). *Wiley Corporate F and A: Supply Chain Transformation: Practical Roadmap to Best Practice Results*. Somerset, NJ, USA: Wiley, p 15.

Sledge, S. (2011). Dynamic competition: a look at firms in the Fortune Global 500, *Competitiveness Review*, Vol. 21 Issue: 5, pp.428 - 440

Soosay, C. A., & Chapman, R. L. (2006). An empirical examination of performance measurement for managing continuous innovation in logistics. *Knowledge and Process Management*, 13(3), 192-205. doi: 10.1002/kpm.257

Spindler, J. (2010). Practice/Distribution of pharmaceutical products pursuant to the 15th AMG amendment - how to combine trading and logistics performance individually. *Pharmazeutische Industrie*, 72(9), 1606-1608.

Timm, N. H. (2002) *Applied Multivariate Analysis*. Secaucus, NJ, USA: Springer. p 477.

Turner, R. W. (2011). *Supply Management and Procurement*. Ft. Lauderdale, FL, USA: J. Ross Publishing Inc., p 176.

World Bank. (2008). *World Trade Indicators, 2008: Benchmarking Policy and Performance*. Herndon, VA, USA: World Bank Publications, p 1-38.

World Bank. (2011). *World Development Indicators: World Development Indicators 2011*. Herndon, VA, USA: World Bank Publications, p 355.

Yan, X. (2009). *Linear Regression Analysis: Theory and Computing*. SGP: World Scientific. p 238.

Appendix

Table A1. Subindex A: Basic requirements

1st pillar: Institutions	3rd pillar: Macroeconomic environment
1.A. Public institutions	3.01 Government budget balance, % GDP
1.01 Property rights	3.02 Gross national savings, % GDP
1.02 Intellectual property protection	3.03 Inflation, annual % change
1.03 Diversion of public funds	3.04 General government debt, % GDP
1.04 Public trust in politicians	3.05 Country credit rating, 0–100 (best)
1.05 Irregular payments and bribes	**4th pillar: Health and primary education**
1.06 Judicial independence	*4. A. Health*
1.07 Favoritism in decisions of government officials	4.01 Business impact of malaria
1.08 Wastefulness of government spending	4.02 Malaria cases/100,000 pop.
1.09 Burden of government regulation	4.03 Business impact of tuberculosis
1.10 Efficiency of legal framework in settling disputes	4.04 Tuberculosis cases/100,000 pop.
1.11 Efficiency of legal framework in challenging regs.	4.05 Business impact of HIV/AIDS
1.12 Transparency of government policymaking	4.06 HIV prevalence, % adult pop.
1.13 Business costs of terrorism	4.07 Infant mortality, deaths/1,000 live births
1.14 Business costs of crime and violence	4.08 Life expectancy, years
1.15 Organized crime	*B. Primary education*
1.16 Reliability of police services	4.09 Quality of primary education
1.B. Private institutions	4.10 Primary education enrollment, net %
1.17 Ethical behavior of firms	
1.18 Strength of auditing and reporting standards	
1.19 Efficacy of corporate boards	
1.20 Protection of minority shareholders' interests	
1.21 Strength of investor protection, 0–10 (best)	
2nd pillar: Infrastructure	
2.A. Transport infrastructure	
2.01 Quality of overall infrastructure	
2.02 Quality of roads	
2.03 Quality of railroad infrastructure	
2.04 Quality of port infrastructure	
2.05 Quality of air transport infrastructure	
2.06 Available airline seat km/week, millions	
2.B. Electricity and telephony infrastructure	
2.07 Quality of electricity supply	
2.08 Mobile telephone subscriptions/100 pop.	
2.09 Fixed telephone lines/100 pop.	

Table A2. Subindex B: Efficiency enhancers

5th pillar: Higher education and training	8th pillar: Financial market development
5.A. Quantity of education	8.A. Efficiency
5.01 Secondary education enrollment, gross	8.01 Availability of financial services
5.02 Tertiary education enrollment, gross %	8.02 Affordability of financial services
5.B. Quality of education	8.03 Financing through local equity market
5.03 Quality of the educational system	8.04 Ease of access to loans
5.04 Quality of math and science education	8.05 Venture capital availability
5.05 Quality of management schools	8.B. Trustworthiness and confidence
5.06 Internet access in schools	8.06 Soundness of banks
5.C. On-the-job training	8.07 Regulation of securities exchanges
5.07 Availability of research and training services	8.08 Legal rights index, 0–10 (best)
5.08 Extent of staff training	**9th pillar: Technological readiness**
6th pillar: Goods market efficiency	*9.A. Technological adoption*
6.A. Competition	9.01 Availability of latest technologies
6.01 Intensity of local competition	9.02 Firm-level technology absorption
6.02 Extent of market dominance	9.03 FDI and technology transfer
6.03 Effectiveness of anti-monopoly policy	*9.B. ICT use*
6.04 Effect of taxation on incentives to invest	9.04 Individuals using Internet, %
6.05 Total tax rate, % profits	9.05 Fixed broadband Internet subscriptions/100 pop.
6.06 No. procedures to start a business	9.06 Int'l Internet bandwidth, kb/s per user
6.07 No. days to start a business	9.07 Mobile broadband subscriptions/100 pop.
6.08 Agricultural policy costs	**10th pillar: Market size**
6.09 Prevalence of trade barriers	*10.A. Domestic market size*
6.10 Trade tariffs, % duty	10.01 Domestic market size index, 1–7 (best)
6.11 Prevalence of foreign ownership	*10.B. Foreign market size*
6.12 Business impact of rules on FDI	10.02 Foreign market size index, 1–7 (best)
6.13 Burden of customs procedures	10.03 GDP (PPP$ billions)
6.14 Imports as a percentage of GDP	10.04 Exports as a percentage of GDP
6.B. Quality of demand conditions	
6.15 Degree of customer orientation	
6.16 Buyer sophistication	
7th pillar: Labor market efficiency	
7.A. Flexibility	
7.01 Cooperation in labor-employer relations	
7.02 Flexibility of wage determination	
7.03 Hiring and firing practices	
7.04 Redundancy costs, weeks of salary	
7.05 Effect of taxation on incentives to work	
7.B. Efficient use of talent	
7.06 Pay and productivity	
7.07 Reliance on professional management	
7.08 Country capacity to retain talent	
7.09 Country capacity to attract talent	
7.10 Women in labor force, ratio to men	

Table A3. Subindex C: Innovation and sophistication factors

11th pillar: Business sophistication
11.01 Local supplier quantity
11.02 Local supplier quality
11.03 State of cluster development
11.04 Nature of competitive advantage
11.05 Value chain breadth
11.06 Control of international distribution
11.07 Production process sophistication
11.08 Extent of marketing
11.09 Willingness to delegate authority
12th pillar: Innovation
12.01 Capacity for innovation
12.02 Quality of scientific research institutions
12.03 Company spending on R&D
12.04 University-industry collaboration in R&D
12.05 Gov't procurement of advanced tech products
12.06 Availability of scientists and engineers
12.07 PCT patents, applications/million pop.

Factor analysis of LPI

The *Kaiser–Meyer–Olkin* measure indicates sampling adequacy, which is 0.938. Since this value is above 0.6, it indicates that sampling is adequate. The *Bartlett's test of sphericity* is a test of the null hypothesis of whether the correlation matrix is an identity matrix, which would indicate that the factor model is inappropriate. Since its P-value is 0.00, which is below the 0.05 threshold, the null hypothesis is rejected. This implies that the model is appropriate for factor analysis.

Table A4. KMO and Bartlett's Test

Kaiser-Meyer-Olkin Measure of Sampling Adequacy.		.938
Bartlett's Test of Sphericity	Approx. Chi-Square	1625.877
	df	15
	Sig.	.000

Table A5. Total variance explained. Extraction method: Principal Component Analysis.

Component	Rotation Sums of Squared Loadings		
	Total	% of Variance	Cumulative %
1	1.035	17.250	17.250
2	1.024	17.072	34.322
3	1.007	16.790	51.112
4	.985	16.417	67.529
5	.984	16.401	83.930
6	.964	16.070	100.000

Table A6. Rotated component matrix[a]

	Component					
	1	2	3	4	5	6
TIME	.692					
ITRN		.677				
CUST			.642			
INFR				.614		
TRAC					.616	
LOGS						.575

Extraction Method: Principal Component Analysis.
Rotation Method: Equamax with Kaiser Normalization.
a. Rotation converged in 59 iterations.

Factor analysis of GCI

The *Kaiser–Meyer–Olkin* measure indicates sampling adequacy, which is 0.902. Since this value is above 0.6, it indicates that sampling is adequate. The *Bartlett's test of sphericity* is a test of the null hypothesis of whether the correlation matrix is an identity matrix, which would indicate that the factor model is inappropriate. Since its P-value is 0.00, which is below the 0.05 threshold, the null hypothesis is rejected. This implies that the model is appropriate for factor analysis.

Table A7. KMO and Bartlett's Test

Kaiser-Meyer-Olkin Measure of Sampling Adequacy.		.902
Bartlett's Test of Sphericity	Approx. Chi-Square	2230.208
	df	66
	Sig.	.000

Table A8. Total variance explained. Extraction method: Principal Component Analysis.

Component	Rotation Sums of Squared Loadings		
	Total	% of Variance	Cumulative %
1	1.143	9.522	9.522
2	1.107	9.224	18.746
3	1.095	9.122	27.868
4	1.093	9.108	36.976
5	1.028	8.568	45.544
6	.952	7.937	53.481
7	.949	7.912	61.393
8	.945	7.875	69.267
9	.933	7.771	77.038
10	.928	7.732	84.770
11	.925	7.711	92.481
12	.902	7.519	100.000

Table A9. Rotated component matrix[a]

	Component											
	1	2	3	4	5	6	7	8	9	10	11	12
10th pillar	.925											
4th pillar		.802										
3rd pillar			.959									
7th pillar				.840								
8th pillar					.750							
6th pillar						.644						
1st pillar							.642					
12th pillar								.616				
9th pillar									.597			
5th pillar										.594		
2nd pillar											.594	
11th pillar												.553

Extraction Method: Principal Component Analysis.
Rotation Method: Equamax with Kaiser Normalization.
a. Rotation converged in 91 iterations.

SEM results for Pillars 1-9:

Table A10. Basic Summary Statistics

	Value
Discrepancy Function	0.303
Maximum Residual Cosine	0.183
Maximum Absolute Gradient	0.070
ICSF Criterion	0.216
ICS Criterion	0.124
ML Chi-Square	39.041
Degrees of Freedom	43.000
p-level	0.644
RMS Standardized Residual	0.040

Table A11. Single Sample Fit Indices

	Value
Joreskog GFI	0.971
Joreskog AGFI	0.918
Akaike Information Criterion	1.496
Schwarz's Bayesian Criterion	3.208
Browne-Cudeck Cross Validation Index	1.665
Independence Model Chi-Square	170.917
Independence Model df	105.000
Bentler-Bonett Normed Fit Index	0.772
Bentler-Bonett Non-Normed Fit Index	1.133
Bentler Comparative Fit Index	1.000
James-Mulaik-Brett Parsimonious Fit Index	0.316
Bollen's Rho	0.442
Bollen's Delta	1.028

Table A12. Measures of Multivariate Kurtosis

	Value
Mardia Coefficient of Multivariate Kurtosis	4.314
Normalized Multivariate Kurtosis	1.089
Mardia-Based Kappa	0.017
Mean Scaled Univariate Kurtosis	0.084
Adjusted Mean Scaled Univariate Kurtosis	0.090
Relative Multivariate Kurtosis	1.017

Table A13. Univariate Skewness Indices

	Skewness	Corrected – Skewness	Normalized – Skewness
PILLAR1	0.142	0.144	0.661
PILLAR2	0.160	0.162	0.743
PILLAR3	-0.011	-0.012	-0.053
PILLAR4	-1.555	-1.573	-7.236
PILLAR5	-0.373	-0.378	-1.738
PILLAR6	-0.592	-0.599	-2.755
PILLAR7	-0.231	-0.234	-1.077
PILLAR8	0.016	0.016	0.075
PILLAR9	0.084	0.085	0.391
TIME	-0.347	-0.351	-1.614
ITRN	-0.378	-0.382	-1.757
CUST	-0.048	-0.049	-0.223
INFR	-0.240	-0.243	-1.116
TRAC	-0.490	-0.496	-2.280
LOGS	-0.607	-0.614	-2.825

Table A14. Univariate Kurtosis Indices

	Kurtosis	Corrected – Kurtosis	Normalized – Kurtosis
PILLAR1	-0.218	-0.179	-0.507
PILLAR2	-0.030	0.016	-0.070
PILLAR3	-0.608	-0.584	-1.414
PILLAR4	2.588	2.738	6.024
PILLAR5	-0.453	-0.423	-1.055
PILLAR6	0.558	0.627	1.298
PILLAR7	-0.017	0.030	-0.039
PILLAR8	0.299	0.358	0.695
PILLAR9	-0.144	-0.102	-0.336
TIME	0.219	0.276	0.511
ITRN	0.003	0.050	0.006
CUST	-0.211	-0.172	-0.491
INFR	0.365	0.427	0.848
TRAC	0.324	0.385	0.755
LOGS	0.262	0.320	0.609

SEM results for Pillars 11-12:

Table A15. Basic Summary Statistics

	Value
Discrepancy Function	0.048
Maximum Residual Cosine	0.000
Maximum Absolute Gradient	0.010
ICSF Criterion	0.000
ICS Criterion	0.000
ML Chi-Square	6.134
Degrees of Freedom	14.000
p-value	0.963
RMS Standardized Residual	0.035

Table A16. Single Sample Fit Indices

	Value
Joreskog GFI	0.988
Joreskog AGFI	0.969
Akaike Information Criterion	0.389
Schwarz's Bayesian Criterion	0.878
Browne-Cudeck Cross Validation Index	0.414
Independence Model Chi-Square	41.096
Independence Model df	28.000
Bentler-Bonett Normed Fit Index	0.851
Bentler-Bonett Non-Normed Fit Index	2.166
Bentler Comparative Fit Index	1.000
James-Mulaik-Brett Parsimonious Fit Index	0.425
Bollen's Rho	0.701
Bollen's Delta	1.285

Table A17. Measures of Multivariate Kurtosis

	Value
Mardia Coefficient of Multivariate Kurtosis	0.626
Normalized Multivariate Kurtosis	0.282
Mardia-Based Kappa	0.008
Mean Scaled Univariate Kurtosis	0.061
Adjusted Mean Scaled Univariate Kurtosis	0.061
Relative Multivariate Kurtosis	1.008

Table A18. Univariate Skewness Indices

	Skewness	Corrected – Skewness	Normalized – Skewness
PILLAR11	-0.018	-0.019	-0.086
PILLAR12	0.599	0.606	2.790
TIME	-0.347	-0.351	-1.614
ITRN	-0.378	-0.382	-1.757
CUST	-0.048	-0.049	-0.223
INFR	-0.240	-0.243	-1.116
TRAC	-0.490	-0.496	-2.280
LOGS	-0.607	-0.614	-2.825

Table A19. Univariate Kurtosis Indices

	Kurtosis	Corrected – Kurtosis	Normalized – Kurtosis
PILLAR11	-0.478	-0.449	-1.112
PILLAR12	0.559	0.629	1.302
TIME	0.219	0.276	0.511
ITRN	0.003	0.050	0.006
CUST	-0.211	-0.172	-0.491
INFR	0.365	0.427	0.848
TRAC	0.324	0.385	0.755
LOGS	0.262	0.320	0.609

Part III
Logistics Performance and Education

Chapter 4. The complex dynamics of the relationship between logistics performance and education

Abstract. Logistics occupations require skills that involve blue- and white-collar activities and different levels of educational skills. With the increase in global trade and competition, the varying skills necessary for different parts of the logistics sector have attracted attention. In this regard, this empirical study examines the relationship between logistics performance indicators and education assessment scores and identifies associations. The presented results, by using canonical correlation analysis, indicate that certain education assessment scores contribute more to improving logistics performance than do other variables. The variables that influence logistics performance are also highlighted.

Keywords: logistics performance, transportation, education assessment, PISA, global competitiveness, canonical correlation

1. Introduction

Logistics professions cover a wide range of skill levels and specialties including equipment operators and mechanics, inventory managers, supply chain managers, business information systems, and distribution frames (Sheffi 2012). To recruit labor and carry out on-the-job training, many logistics groups attract and develop workers in partnership with educational institutions that supply vocational, undergraduate, postgraduate, and professional training (Sheffi 2012).

Although logistics may seem like a blue-collar task of moving boxes and driving trucks, it encompasses much more (Sheffi 2012). Indeed, white-collar jobs provide almost 25% of logistics jobs: office and administrative support (including stock clerks, dispatchers, customer service representatives, and office workers) account for 17% of labor in the industry, management, business, and finance positions 4%, and frontline supervisors 3% (Sheffi 2012). With the increase in global trade and efficiency requirements come rising demand for professionals with knowledge on supply chain management (SCM), including storage, transport, supply, distribution, vendor management, and IT processes (Sheffi 2012).

Technological, economic, and political trends have increased demand for higher skills and reduced demand for low skills while increasing competition for quality jobs (Stewart 2012). This is one reason for paying attention to the international assessments that have recently been implemented. These evaluations and their results have led to a growing body of research, observation, and discussion that goes beyond the numbers and rankings to help us understand why some systems are moving forward quickly and producing more equitable performance, while others remain static and uneven (Stewart 2012).

The current research was undertaken to address the issue of developing human capital in the field of logistics, specifically for achieving higher logistics performance. In which areas, do logistics firms need help building competencies in order to improve performance? What skills should these firms be looking for in the first place? More specifically, how do education and skills influence logistics performance?

The remainder of this study is organized as follows. Section 2 reviews the literature on logistics in general and education-related issues in particular. Section 3 introduces the data and methods used for the canonical correlation analyses of the perceptions of countries' logistics efficiencies and educational scores by using various measures drawn from the World Bank, the Global Competitiveness Index (GCI) of the World Economic Forum (WEF), and the International Institute for Management Development (IMD) database. Specifically, this section investigates the associations between logistics performance indicators and education-related scores derived from the Programme for International Student Assessment (PISA) of the OECD, the WEF, and the IMD. In addition, ridge regression analysis is performed on the logistics performance indicators and PISA education variables to find those variables that contribute most to influencing overall logistics performance. Section 4 presents and discusses the empirical findings. The study is concluded in Section 5.

2. Literature review

Koenig (2011) stated that there is a growing recognition that individuals need a broad range of skills to meet the demands of the modern workplace. Gone are the days where multitudes of jobs were available that required workers to perform simple manual tasks (Koenig 2011). In this vein, Goldsby and Martichenko (2005) indicated that all forms of education continue to offer the fastest return on the investment made and that all knowledge acquired through training exercises improves firm performance.

Svensson (2007) stated that logistics educators in general have received their training in marketing, operations, and quantitative methods, but that skills in organizational behavior and psychology are also required. These skill sets suggest that current teachers are ill equipped to deal with the new managerial dimensions required for modern SCM (Svensson 2007). However, these additional dimensions must be incorporated into logistics education if the promises of SCM are to be met (Svensson 2007). Managers should also search out such educational opportunities.

The rapid expansion of national participation in studies of international achievement has been a feature of education planning over the past 25 years

(Wiseman 2010). Large-scale international comparative educational assessments began more than 50 years ago with the formation of the International Association for the Evaluation of Educational Achievement (IEA) and they have since developed and diversified (Wiseman 2010). However, particularly over the past decade, renewed interest in these studies has swept public discourse. National rankings of test results are now part of common educational jargon and the number, severity, scope, complexity, and connectivity of these assessments are at an historically high level (Wiseman 2010).

Researchers have examined the connection between industry performance and education on SCM. For example, authors have explored the challenges of SCM module boards (Bak and Boulocher-Passet 2013), the development of SCM training (Bernon and Mena 2013), using SCM software in education (Campbell *et al.* 2000.), the integration of production and logistics in principle, in practice, and in education (Chikan 2001), and education and training needs in logistics (Felea *et al.* 2010). Furthermore, scholars have investigated logistics and SCM doctoral training (Grant and Bourlakis 2010), SCM simulation as a tool for education (Holweg and Bicheno 2002), and SCM for education engineering students and employees (Ilie-Zudor *et al.* 2011).

Research on logistics education has also examined the current state of the art (Lutz and Birou 2013), using SCM to improve collaboration between universities (Om *et al.* 2007), and the future of education logistics (Ozment and Keller 2011). Similarly, previous studies have explored activities and education in logistics (Skrinjar *et al.* 2008), competitiveness, manufacturing, and the role of education in SCM in the forest industry (Smith 2005), the provision of education and current practitioner future needs (van Hoek and Wagner 2013), and competitiveness, manufacturing, and the role of education (Winistörfer 2005).

The modern workplace requires workers to have broad cognitive and affective skills (Koenig 2011), often referred to as "21st century skills." These skills include being able to solve complex problems, think critically about tasks, communicate effectively with people of different cultures, use a variety of techniques, work with others, adapt to changing environments and conditions to carry out tasks, effectively manage workload, and acquire new skills and information proactively (Koenig 2011). Skills, which relate to experience and are knowledge context-dependent, are taught in most logistics classes, which are vital for practitioners (Gammelgaard and Larson 2001). However, to achieve a level of competence in the discipline of logistics, practitioners gain knowledge depending on their degrees of organizational experience (Gammelgaard and Larson 2001).

The present study adds another dimension to the existing literature. In this regard, by using statistical methods, it provides a better understanding for policymakers. Specifically, it differs from previous works in that it investigates statistically significant relationships between logistics performance and education assessment scores.

3. Data and methods

In this study, four main types of data sources are used, all of which are drawn from the World Bank, the GCI database, and the IMD's World Competitiveness database. The first data source is on the perceptions of countries' logistics efficiencies. The second data source is the PISA survey assessment indicators. The third data source is the fifth pillar from the GCI (GCI5 hereafter), which measures higher education and training. The fourth data source is the IMD's various education scores (see Tables A17 and A18).

The Logistics Performance Index (LPI) is the first international benchmarking tool that measures the ease of trade and transport logistics by country (McLinden *et al.* 2010). The LPI is based on a global survey that the World Bank conducts every two years, covering 155 countries and completed by nearly 1,000 logistics professionals in international freight forwarders and express carriers (Arvis *et al.* 2010). Each LPI report contains a comprehensive cross-country assessment to help countries identify their challenges and opportunities in trade and transport logistics performance and disaggregates data into six categories to highlight problem areas (McLinden *et al.* 2010).

The composite LPI summarizes all areas of performance. In brief, these variables are as follows: CUST stands for the customs clearance process, INFR is the quality of trade and transport-related infrastructure, ITRN is the ease of arranging competitively priced shipments, LOGS is the quality of logistics services, TRAC is the ability to track and trace consignments, TIME is the frequency with which shipments reach the consignee within the scheduled time, and OVRL is overall logistics performance.

PISA is a triennial international survey that aims to evaluate education systems worldwide by testing the skills and knowledge of 15-year-olds. To date, students representing over 70 countries have participated in the evaluation. PISA 2012, the fifth survey program, assessed the skills of 15-year-olds in reading (READ), mathematics (MATH), and science (SCI) in 65 countries and economies. Approximately 510,000 students aged 15 years and 3 months and 16 years and 2 months participated in the evaluation, which represents about 28 million children worldwide, thereby providing evidence of the effect of the development of younger children on later school success (Wu *et al.* 2012). PISA is unique because it develops tests that are not directly related to the curriculum. These tests are designed to assess how well students at the end of compulsory education can apply their knowledge to real-life situations and be equipped to participate fully in society. The information gathered through questionnaires also provides a context that can help analysts interpret the results.

The GCI (2013–2014) measured national competitiveness by using a complex methodology involving raw data and executive opinions. The index rests on 12 pillars categorized into three groups, namely *basic requirements* (four pillars), *efficiency enhancers* (six pillars), and *innovation and sophistication factors* (two pillars). Countries are rated on a seven-point scale, with a higher score indicating more competitiveness. In this research, the fifth pillar, which concerns *higher education and training*, is taken into consideration. This pillar has three sub indicators: *quantity of education*, *quality of education*, and *on-the-job training*.

The GCI is a comprehensive database of the competitiveness of nations. Global competitiveness is an area of economic theory that analyzes the facts and policies that shape the ability of a nation to create and maintain an environment that sustains more value creation for its enterprises and more prosperity for its people. The approach of the IMD's World Competitiveness Center for global competitiveness is to analyze how nations and businesses manage all their skills to achieve greater prosperity. From this database, only education-related variables are used in this study.

It should be noted that the LPI variables (CUST, INFR, ITRN, LOGS, TRAC, TIME) introduce severe multicollinearity. Multicollinearity, which occurs when the predictors included in the linear model are highly correlated (Yan 2009), poses statistical inference problems. Therefore, to overcome this problem, by applying the factor analysis technique, six LPI variables were factor analyzed and six components extracted, each representing their respective variables, although factor analysis mainly aims to obtain a smaller number of factors that account for most of the variability. In this special case, six factors were extracted from the six variables. Together, they accounted for 100% of the variability in the original LPI data. Finally, these extracted factors were stored as Anderson–Rubin factor scores, which are uncorrelated scores with other factors. The same multicollinearity issue for the three PISA variables (MATH, READ, SCI) was also overcome by using the same technique. The factor loadings of the equamax rotation are presented in Tables A1 through A6.

Multicollinearity does not pose a problem for the GCI5 variables. The preliminary tests of these variables indicated that the variance inflation factors (VIFs) were below 5. VIF is an indicator of how the other explanatory variables affect the variance of a regression coefficient of a particular variable, given by the inverse of the square of the multiple correlation coefficient of the variable with the remaining variables (Everitt 2002). Ideally, researchers are looking for VIFs<10 (see Table A7). The multicollinearity issue was overcome for the IMD variables by extracting factor scores and storing the extracted factors as Anderson–Rubin factor scores (see Tables A11 through A16).

3.1 Canonical correlation analysis of logistics performance indicators and PISA scores

Nearly 80 years ago, Harold Hotelling (1936) introduced canonical correlation analysis (see also Brown *et al.* 2011). Essentially, this method identifies the holistic relationship between two multivariate sets of variables, an obvious next step after factor analysis and principal component analysis made their appearance in the first decades of the twentieth century (Brown *et al.* 2011). This procedure finds the linear combinations of two sets of variables that have the highest correlation between them (see Table A8 for the linear relationship between the LPI and PISA scores).

Table 1. Chi-Square tests with successive roots removed. Rows having p<0.05 are highlighted.

	Canonical R	Canonical R-sqr.	Chi-sqr.	df	p	Lambda – Prime
0	0.72	0.52	56.62	18	0.00	0.33
1	0.51	0.26	18.66	10	0.04	0.69
2	0.24	0.06	2.97	4	0.56	0.94

The canonical analysis summary is that the canonical R equals 0.72, Chi²(57) equals 56.61, and p equals 0.00. In this case, three sets of linear combinations have been formed. However, only two sets are statistically significant (p<0.05; Table 1 and Figure 1). The first set, which forms the strongest correlations, has the following highly contributing variables:

$U_1 = -0.68 \times \mathbf{MATH} - 0.55 \times \text{READ} - 0.46 \times \text{SCI}$

and

$L_1 = -0.61 \times \mathbf{CUST} - 0.36 \times \text{INFR} - 0.39 \times \text{ITRN} - 0.47 \times \mathbf{LOGS} - 0.09 \times \text{TIME} - 0.16 \times \text{TRAC}$

In addition, the second set of linear combinations, the next strongest correlation among all combinations that are uncorrelated with the first set, has the following highlighted highly contributing variables:

$U_2 = -0.43 \times \text{MATH} + \mathbf{0.83 \times READ} - 0.38 \times \text{SCI}$

and

$L_2 = -0.07 \times \text{CUST} + 0.45 \times \text{INFR} - 0.25 \times \text{ITRN} - 0.30 \times \text{LOGS} + \mathbf{0.95 \times TIME} + \mathbf{0.67 \times TRAC}$

where the variables have first been standardized by subtracting their means and dividing by their standard deviations. Table 1 and Figure 1 show the estimated correlations between each set of canonical variables. Since two of the p values are less than 0.05, those sets have statistically significant correlations at the 95% confidence level.

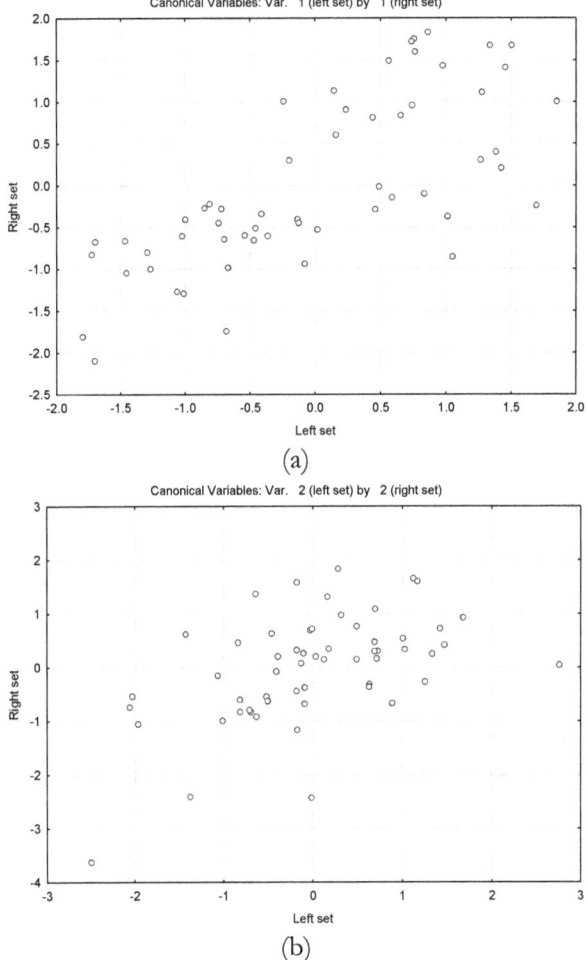

Figure 1. (a) PISA (right set root 1) versus LPI (left set root 1) and (b) PISA (right set root 2) versus LPI (left set root 2)

Other ways of dealing with complex sets of multivariate data are structural equation modeling and confirmatory factor analysis (Brown *et al.* 2011). These powerful developments in the factor analytic tradition, which have arrived over the past three decades or so, constitute a computational general case of which factor analysis and canonical correlation analysis are special cases (Brown *et al.* 2011). Whereas principal component analysis, canonical correlation analysis, and some factor analyses can improve the holistic understanding of complex data and provide a better visible apprehension of one's data, structural equation models allow researchers to test specific scientific models against complex empirical data (Brown *et al.* 2011).

3.2 Ridge regression for logistics performance indicators versus raw PISA scores

Ridge regression is one of the remedies to treat severe multicollinearity in least squares estimations (Yan 2009). One approach to dealing with multicollinearity is thus to apply the ridge regression (Lesaffre and Lawson 2012). The method of ridge regression suggested by Hoerl in 1962 and systematically developed by Hoerl and Kennard (1970a, 1970b) can significantly improve the mean squared error of the least squares estimator when the columns of the matrix vector design are multicollinear (Tong *et al.* 2011).

The R-Squared statistic indicates that the model as fitted explains 46.32% of the variability in OVRL. The adjusted R-Squared statistic, which is more suitable for comparing models with different numbers of independent variables, is 43.28%. The standard error of the estimate shows the standard deviation of the residuals to be 0.35. The mean absolute error of 0.28 is the average value of the residuals. The Durbin–Watson statistic tests the residuals to determine if there is any significant correlation based on the order in which they occur in the data.

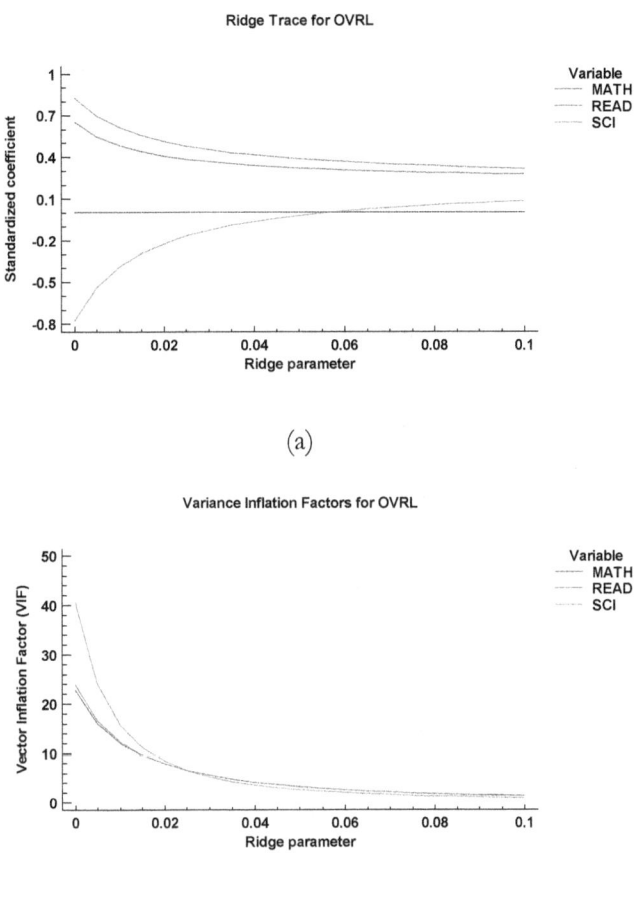

Figure 2. (a) Ridge trace for OVRL and (b) VIFs for OVRL

Figure 2a shows the standardized regression coefficients for the values of the ridge parameter between 0.0 and 0.1. These are the coefficients of the regression model when the variables are expressed in standardized form. As the ridge parameter increases from 0, the coefficients often change dramatically at first and then become relatively stable. A good value for the ridge parameter is the smallest value after which the estimates change slowly. This is admittedly subjective, but the ridge trace helps researchers make a good choice.

Figure 2b shows the VIFs for each of the coefficients in the regression model. VIFs measure the degree to which the variance of the estimated coefficients is inflated relative to the case when all the independent variables are uncorrelated. As before, as the ridge parameter increases from 0, the VIFs often decrease dramatically at first and then become relatively stable. A good value for the ridge parameter is also the smallest value after which the VIFs change slowly. This is admittedly subjective, but the plot of the VIFs again helps us make a good choice.

This procedure aims to estimate the regression coefficients when the independent variables are strongly correlated. By allowing for a small amount of bias, the precision of these estimates can often be greatly increased. In this case, the fitted regression model is

OVRL = 0.3593 + **0.0025×MATH** + **0.0032×READ** + 0.0008×SCI

Table 2. Model results when the ridge parameter is 0.1.

Parameter	Estimate	VIFs
Constant	0.3593	
MATH	0.0025	1.32968
READ	0.0032	1.30215
SCI	0.0008	0.911942

3.3 Canonical correlation analysis of logistics performance indicators and GCI5 scores

As noted earlier, this procedure finds the linear combinations of two sets of variables that have the highest correlation between them (see Table A9 for the linear relationship between the LPI and GCI5). The canonical analysis summary is that the canonical R equals 0.87, $Chi^2(18)$ equals 189.45, and p equals 0.00.

Table 3. Chi-Square tests with successive roots removed. Rows having $p<0.05$ are highlighted.

	Canonical R	Canonical R-sqr.	Chi-sqr.	df	p	Lambda – Prime
0	0.87	0.75	189.45	18	0.00	0.21
1	0.30	0.09	19.61	10	0.03	0.85
2	0.25	0.06	7.71	4	0.10	0.94

In this case, three sets of linear combinations have been formed. However, only two sets are statistically significant (p<0.05; Table 3 and Figure 3). The first set forms the strongest correlations (R^2 equals 0.75). In detail, the first set of linear combinations with the highlighted highly contributing variables is

U_3 = +0.43×F_TIME + 0.31×F_ITRN + 0.42×F_CUST + 0.35×F_INFR + **0.50×F_TRAC** + 0.37×F_LOGS

and

L_3 = +0.37×[Quantity of education] − 0.01×[Quality of education] + **0.76×[On-the-job training]**

The second set of linear combinations, which has the next strongest correlation (R^2 equals 0.09) among all combinations that are uncorrelated with the first set, has the following contributing variables:

U_4 = −0.25×F_TIME + 0.17×F_ITRN − **0.76×F_CUST** + **0.51×F_INFR** + 0.20×F_TRAC + 0.27×F_LOGS

and

L_4 = +0.72×[Quantity of education] − **2.01×[Quality of education]** + 1.23×[On-the-job training]

where the variables have first been standardized by subtracting their means and dividing by their standard deviations. Table 3 and Figure 3 show the estimated correlations between each set of canonical variables. Since two of the p values are less than 0.05, those sets have statistically significant correlations at the 95% confidence level.

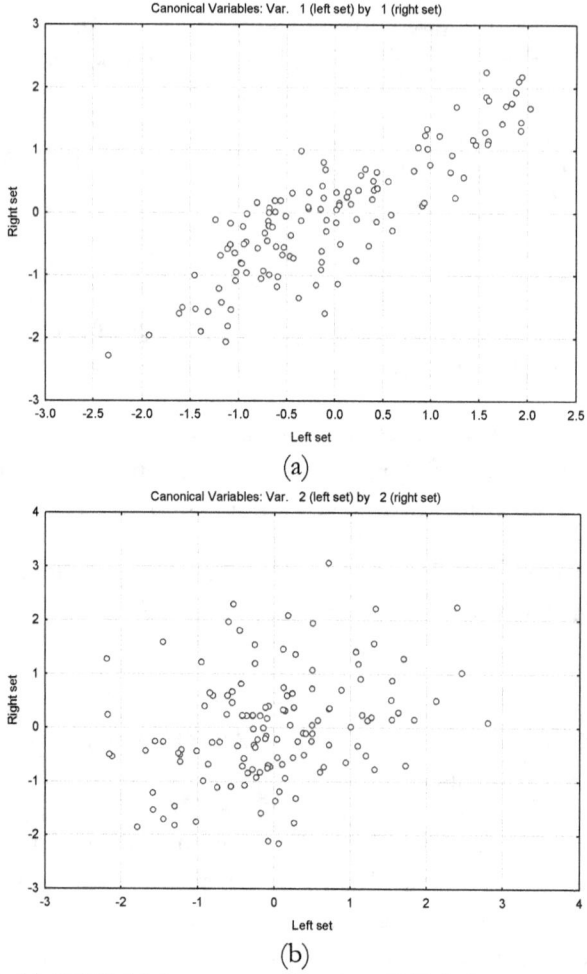

Figure 3. (a) GCI5 (right set root 1) versus LPI (left set root 1) and (b) GCI5 (right set root 2) versus LPI (left set root 2)

3.4 Canonical correlation analysis of logistics performance indicators and IMD scores

Again, this procedure finds the linear combinations of two sets of variables that have the highest correlations between them (see Table 4 for the linear relationship between the LPI and the IMD's education assessment pillar). The canonical analysis summary is that the canonical R equals 0.98, $Chi^2(96)$ equals 135.18, and p equals 0.00.

Table 4. Chi-Square tests with successive roots removed. Rows having p<0.05 are highlighted.

	Canonical R	Canonical R-sqr.	Chi-sqr.	df	p	Lambda – Prime
0	0.98	0.97	135.18	96	0.01	0.00
1	0.95	0.90	82.76	75	0.25	0.00
2	0.87	0.75	46.64	56	0.81	0.05

In this case, some sets of linear combinations have been formed. However, only one set of linear combinations is statistically significant (p<0.05; Table 4 and Figure 4). The first set forms the strongest correlations (R^2 equals 0.97) and this has the following highly contributing variables:

U_5 = **–0.45×[Student mobility outbound]**
– 0.13×[Educational assessment, Science]
–0.11×[Language skills]
– 0.10×[Pupil-teacher ratio (primary education)]
–0.03×[Secondary school enrollment (%)]
– 0.02×[Total public expenditure on education]
+0.02×[Management education] + 0.03×[Educational assessment, Mathematics]
+0.17×[English proficiency - TOEFL] + 0.19×[Student mobility inbound]
+0.22×[Higher education achievement (%)] + 0.24×[Pupil-teacher ratio (secondary education)]
+0.31×[Educational system] + 0.33×[Illiteracy (%)]
+0.41×[University education] + 0.55×[Science in schools]

and

L_5 = –0.22×F_INFR–0.12×F_TIME + 0.17×F_LOGS + 0.18×F_ITRN + **0.46×F_CUST + 0.82×F_TRAC**

where the variables have first been standardized by subtracting their means and dividing by their standard deviations. Table 4 and Figure 4 show the estimated correlations between each set of canonical variables. Since two of the p values are less than 0.05, those sets have statistically significant correlations at the 95% confidence level.

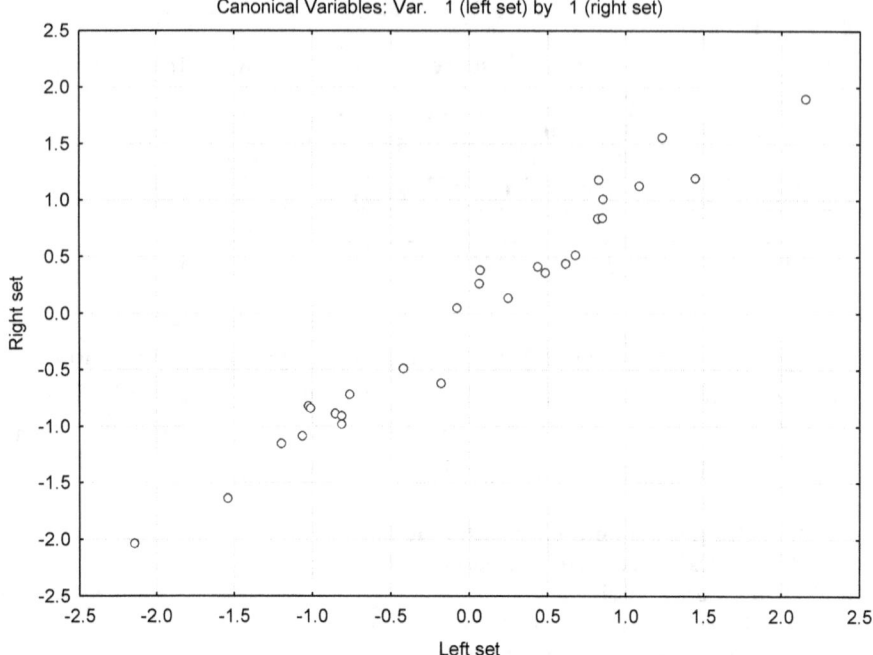

Figure 4. IMD scores (left set root 1) versus LPI (right set root 1)

4. Findings and discussion

The first canonical correlation, U_1 and L_1, is moderately strong with a magnitude of 0.72 and statistically significant at $p<0.05$ (see Table 1 and Figure 1a). There are primarily relationships between the logistics performance variables of LOGS and CUST, on the one hand, and the education assessment variable of MATH with some contribution from READ and SCI, on the other. This finding implies that *the quality of logistics services* and *customs clearance process* are related to the education assessment variables of the *mathematics* skill, with some contribution from the *reading* and *science* skills.

The second canonical correlation, U_2 and L_2, is less strong with a magnitude of 0.51 and statistically significant at $p<0.05$ (Table 1 and Figure 1b). We see relationships between the logistics performance variables of TIME and TRAC and the education assessment variable of READ with some contribution from MATH and SCI. The implication here is that *the frequency with which shipments reach the consignee within the scheduled time* and *the ability to track and trace consignments* are related to the education assessment variable of the *reading* skill with some contribution from the *mathematics* and *science* skills.

The ridge regression model for the dependent variable of OVRL versus the PISA variables shows the contributions of the independent variables. The R-Squared statistic indicates that the model as fitted explains 46.32% of the variability in OVRL. The adjusted R-Squared statistic, which is more suitable for comparing models with different numbers of independent variables, is 43.28% and is moderately strong (Table 2). As the fitted ridge regression model explains, the MATH and READ variables highly contribute to overall logistics performance with a smaller coefficient of SCI.

For GCI5 versus the LPI variables, the first canonical correlation, U_3 and L_3, is moderately strong with a magnitude of 0.87 and statistically significant at $p<0.05$ (Table 3 and Figure 3a). There seems to be a relationship between all logistics performance variables (as their coefficients are close to each other) and the education assessment variable of *On-the-job training* with some contribution from *Quantity of education*. Primarily, TRAC and the variable *On-the-job training* are canonically correlated with the highest coefficient. This finding implies that *the ability to track and trace consignments* is primarily related to the education assessment variable of the *On-the-job training* with some contribution from *Quantity of education*. *Quality of education* has almost no effect in this first canonical correlation.

The second canonical correlation of GCI5 versus the LPI variables, U_4 and L_4, is less strong with a magnitude of 0.51 and statistically significant at $p<0.05$ (Table 3 and Figure 3b). There is a relationship between CUST and INFR and the education assessment variable of *Quality of education* with some contribution from *On-the-job training* and *Quantity of education*. The primary implication here is that *the customs clearance process* and *quality of trade and transport-related infrastructure* are related to the *Quality of education* with some contribution from *On-the-job training* and *Quantity of education*.

For the IMD versus the LPI variables, the canonical correlation, U_5 and L_5, is strong with a magnitude of 0.98 and statistically significant at $p<0.05$ (Table 4 and Figure 4). CUST and TRAC are related to science education in schools and university education with some contribution from illiteracy (percentage) and the educational system. This finding implies that the *ability to track and trace consignments* and *customs clearance process* are related to the education assessment variables of *Science education in schools* and *university education* with some contribution from *illiteracy (percentage)* and the *educational system*.

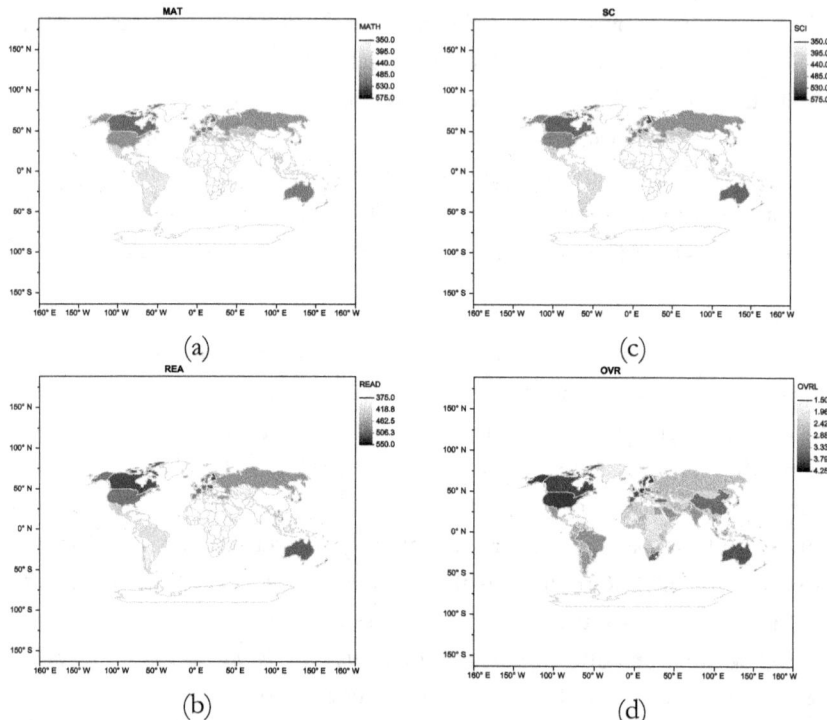

Figure 4. In each figure, the countries with darker (lighter) grays indicate good (poor) performance. White regions/countries: unavailable data. (a) MATH scores, (b) READ scores, (c) SCI scores, and (d) overall logistics performance (OVRL)

All countries are trying to get people out of poverty and respond to increasing public pressure to provide more economic opportunities for the next generation through the expansion of education (Stewart 2012). Countries with high performance and rapid improvement are also carefully designed as learning systems, constantly checking and updating in order to determine if the education system is preparing their students for the knowledge economy in this rapidly changing world (Stewart 2012). However, during the past two decades, countries have focused on the expansion of education as the key driver to maximizing individual well-being, reducing poverty, and stimulating economic growth (Stewart 2012) (see Figures 4, 5, and 6).

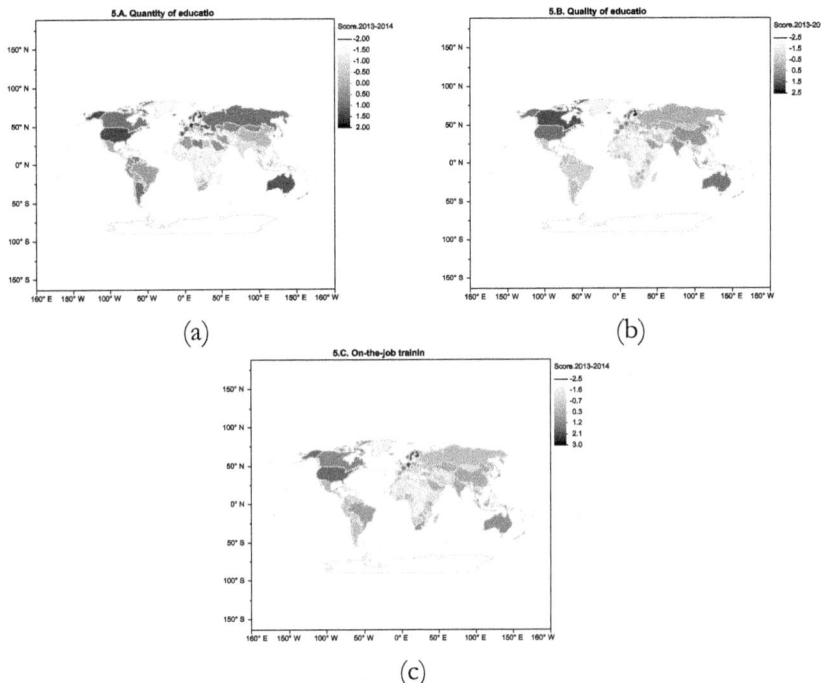

Figure 5. (a) Quantity of education scores, (b) Quality of education scores, and (c) On-the-job training scores

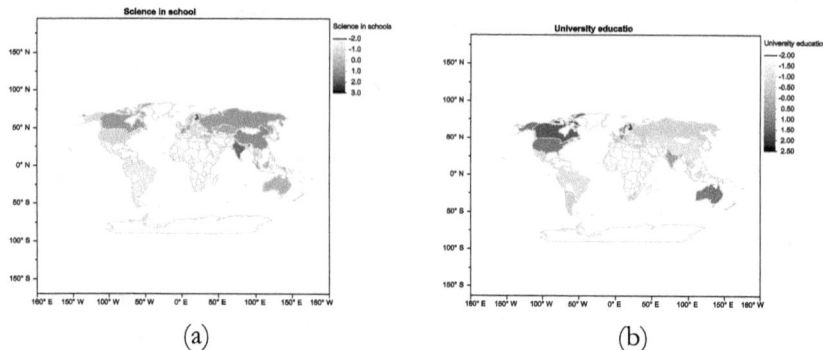

Figure 6. (a) Science in schools and (b) University education. Source: the IMD World Competitiveness database (60 countries)

The design, management, and constant renewal of logistics systems and the supply chain demand considerable sophistication and analytical knowledge (Sheffi 2012). The analysis of logistics systems makes extensive use of mathematics, particularly operations research methods that aim to optimize the flow of goods, people, and goods subject to the constraints of cost, time, capacity, and uncertainty (Sheffi 2012). Even though a worker can physically move a box, intellectual muscle remains necessary in order to determine which of the thousands of boxes to put in which truck to transport each item (Sheffi 2012). Because tasks such as designing a network of distribution centers, planning travel modes, and optimizing inventory in the face of an uncertain future need technical sophistication, companies require logistics managers and engineers with university and postgraduate training (Sheffi 2012).

Globalization poses challenges for everyone. Every education system in the world is struggling to some extent to deal with the rapid pace of change (Stewart 2012). In addition, countries are facing similar challenges. For example, internal and international migration have created more widespread heterogeneous societies everywhere, imposing new demands on teachers as they respond to students and families from diverse cultural and linguistic backgrounds (Stewart 2012).

5. Conclusion

In this empirical study, we examined the relationship between logistics performance indicators and educational assessment scores and identified associations. The presented results indicated that certain educational assessment indicators, as evidenced by the canonical correlation analyses, contribute much more to improving logistics performance than do other variables. In this regard, it is essential for policymakers in the logistics sector to take account of those variables that have higher contributions in order to improve outcomes significantly.

This research has one main limitation, as it does not directly assess the group of skills required to improve logistics performance. It rather investigated the canonical correlations between logistics performance and selected educational assessment scores, which is an indirect measurement of contribution. However, as the assessment scores suggest, countries that provide better education opportunities are also those that improve logistics performance. Further research should nevertheless aim to investigate those skills directly related to the logistics industry that can improve logistics performance. Such research would shed light on the primary skills needed in the logistics sector.

6. References

Arvis, J. F., Marteau, J. F., & Raballand, G. (2010) *'Directions in Development: Cost of Being Landlocked: Logistics Costs and Supply Chain Reliability'*, Herndon, VA, USA: World Bank Publications. p xi-77.

Bak, O., & Boulocher-Passet, V. (2013). Connecting industry and supply chain management education: exploring challenges faced in a SCM consultancy module. *Supply Chain Management – An International Journal*, 18(4), 468-479. doi: 10.1108/scm-11-2012-0357

Bernon, M., & Mena, C. (2013). The evolution of customised executive education in supply chain management. *Supply Chain Management – An International Journal*, 18(4), 440-454. doi: 10.1108/scm-07-2012-0262

Brown, B. L., Hendrix, S. B., Hedges, D. W. (2011). *Multivariate Analysis for the Biobehavioral and Social Sciences: A Graphical Approach*. Hoboken, NJ, USA: Wiley, 2011. p 297-328.

Campbell, A., Goentzel, J., & Savelsbergh, M. (2000). Experiences with the use of supply chain management software in education. *Production and Operations Management*, 9(1), 66-80.

Chikan, A. (2001). Integration of production and logistics - in principle, in practice and in education. *International Journal of Production Economics*, 69(2), 129-140. doi: 10.1016/s0925-5273(99)00102-4

Everitt, B. S. (2002). *Cambridge Dictionary of Statistics*. West Nyack, NY, USA: Cambridge University Press, p 325-389.

Felea, M., Yankov, N., Maruntelu, I., & Vasiliu, C. (2010). Education and training needs in the field of logistic structures and services in the lower Danube region. *Amfiteatru Economic*, 12, 785-814.

Gammelgaard, B., & Larson, P. D. (2001). Logistics skills and competencies for supply chain management. *Journal of Business Logistics*, 22(2), 27-50. doi: 10.1002/j.2158-1592.2001.tb00002.x

Goldsby, T. J., Martichenko, R. (2005). *Lean Six Sigma Logistics*. Boca Raton, FL, USA: J. Ross Publishing, Incorporated, p 76.

Grant, D. B., & Bourlakis, M. (2010). Comment on logistics and SCM doctoral education: the European logistics association doctorate workshop. *International Journal of Logistics-Research and Applications*, 13(2), 97-98. doi: 10.1080/13675560903557817

Hoerl, A.E., Kennard, R. W. (1970a). Ridge regression: Applications to nonorthogonal problems. *Technometrics*, 12:69– 82.

Hoerl, A.E., Kennard, R. W. (1970b). Ridge regression: Biased estimation for nonorthogonal problems. *Technometrics*, 12:55– 67.

Hoerl, A.E. (1962). Application of ridge analysis to regression problems, *Chemical Engineering Progress*, 1958, 54–59.

Holweg, M., & Bicheno, J. (2002). Supply chain simulation – A tool for education, enhancement and endeavour. *International Journal of Production Economics*, 78(2), 163-175. doi: 10.1016/s0925-5273(00)00171-7

Hotelling, H. (1936). Relations between two sets of variates. *Biometrika*, 28, 321– 377.

Ilie-Zudor, E., Macchi, M., Monostori, L., Scotti, S., & Kemeny, Z. (2011). Engineering Education on Supply-Chain Management for Students and for Employees in Industry. *Computer Applications in Engineering Education*, 19(1), 81-88. doi: 10.1002/cae.20293

Koenig, J. A. (2011). *Assessing 21st Century Skills: Summary of a Workshop*. Washington, DC, USA: National Academies Press. p 1.

Lesaffre, E., Lawson, A. B. (2012). *Statistics in Practice: Bayesian Biostatistics.* Somerset, NJ, USA: Wiley. p 209.

Lutz, H., & Birou, L. (2013). Logistics education: a look at the current state of the art and science. *Supply Chain Management-An International Journal,* 18(4), 455-467. doi: 10.1108/scm-08-2012-0269

McLinden, G. (Editor), Fanta, E. (Editor), Widdowson, D. (Editor). (2010). *Border Management Modernization.* Herndon, VA, USA: World Bank Publications. p 24.

Om, K., Lee, J., & Chang, J. (2007). Using supply chain management to enhance industry-university collaborations in IT higher education in Korea. *Scientometrics,* 71(3), 455-471. doi: 10.1007/s11192-007-1690-3

Ozment, J., & Keller, S. B. (2011). The Future of Logistics Education. *Transportation Journal,* 50(1), 65-83.

Sheffi, Y. (2012). *Logistics Clusters: Delivering Value and Driving Growth.* Cambridge, MA, USA: MIT Press. p 209-220.

Skrinjar, J. P., Ivakovic, C., & Simunovic, L. (2008). Activities and education in logistics. *Promet-Traffic & Transportation,* 20(2), 125-132.

Smith, W. R. (2005). Competitiveness, manufacturing, and the role of education in the supply chain for the forest industry. *Forest Products Journal,* 55(6), 1-1.

Stewart, V. (2012). *World-Class Education: Learning from International Models of Excellence and Innovation.* Alexandria, VA, USA: Association for Supervision & Curriculum Development (ASCD). p 1-35.

Svensson, G. (Editor). (2007). *European Business Review,* Volume 19, Issue 4: Current Status and Future Direction: Views From Global Thought Leaders II. Bradford, GBR: Emerald Group Publishing Ltd. p 346.

Tong, H, Kumar, T. K., Huang, Y. (2011). *Developing Econometrics.* Hoboken, NJ, USA: Wiley. p 68.

van Hoek, R., & Wagner, B. (2013). Supply chain management (SCM): current education provision and practitioner future needs. *Supply Chain Management-An International Journal,* 18(4), 355-357. doi: 10.1108/scm-05-2013-0159

Winistorfer, P. M. (2005). Competitiveness, manufacturing, and the role of education in the supply chain for the forest industry. *Forest Products Journal,* 55(6), 6-16.

Wiseman, A. W. (Editor). (2010). *International Perspectives on Education and Society,* Volume 13: The Impact of International Achievement Studies on

National Education Policymaking. Bradford, GBR: Emerald Group Publishing Ltd. p 13-321.

Wu, K. B., Young, M. E., Cai, J. (2012). *Early Childhood Development and Education in China: Breaking the Cycle of Poverty and Improving Future Competitiveness*. Herndon, VA, USA: World Bank Publications. p xxiv.

Yan, X. (2009). *Linear Regression Analysis: Theory and Computing*. SGP: World Scientific. p 238.

Appendix

Factor analysis of LPI and PISA scores

Retrieval of LPI Factors:

The *Kaiser–Meyer–Olkin* measure indicates sampling adequacy, which is 0.938. Since this value is above 0.6, it indicates that sampling is adequate. *Bartlett's test of sphericity* is a test of the null hypothesis of whether the correlation matrix is an identity matrix, which would indicate that the factor model is inappropriate. Since its P-value is 0.00, which is below the 0.05 threshold, the null hypothesis is rejected. This implies that the model is appropriate for factor analysis.

Table A1. KMO and Bartlett's Test

Kaiser-Meyer-Olkin Measure of Sampling Adequacy.		.938
Bartlett's Test of Sphericity	Approx. Chi-Square	1625.877
	df	15
	Sig.	.000

Table A2. Total variance explained. Extraction method: Principal Component Analysis.

Component	Rotation Sums of Squared Loadings		
	Total	% of Variance	Cumulative %
1	1.035	17.250	17.250
2	1.024	17.072	34.322
3	1.007	16.790	51.112
4	.985	16.417	67.529
5	.984	16.401	83.930
6	.964	16.070	100.000

Table A3. Rotated component matrix[a]

	1	2	3	4	5	6
TIME	.692					
ITRN		.677				
CUST			.642			
INFR				.614		
TRAC					.616	
LOGS						.575

Extraction Method: Principal Component Analysis.
Rotation Method: Equamax with Kaiser Normalization.
a. Rotation converged in 59 iterations.

Retrieval of PISA Factors:

The *Kaiser–Meyer–Olkin* measure indicates sampling adequacy, which is 0.761. Since this value is above 0.6, it indicates that sampling is adequate. *Bartlett's test of sphericity* is a test of the null hypothesis of whether the correlation matrix is an identity matrix, which would indicate that the factor model is inappropriate. Since its P-value is 0.00, which is below the 0.05 threshold, the null hypothesis is rejected. This implies that the model is appropriate for factor analysis.

Table A4. KMO and Bartlett's Test

Kaiser-Meyer-Olkin Measure of Sampling Adequacy.		.761
Bartlett's Test of Sphericity	Approx. Chi-Square	353.298
	df	3
	Sig.	.000

Table A5. Total variance explained. Extraction method: Principal Component Analysis.

Component	Rotation Sums of Squared Loadings		
	Total	% of Variance	Cumulative %
1	1.016	33.857	33.857
2	1.008	33.592	67.449
3	.977	32.551	100.000

Table A6. Rotated component matrix[a]

	Component		
	1	2	3
MATH	.699		
READ		.691	
SCI			.656

Extraction Method: Principal Component Analysis.
Rotation Method: Equamax with Kaiser Normalization.
a. Rotation converged in 36 iterations.

Table A7. VIFs and coefficients[a] of fifth pillar of GCI variables.

Model	Standardized Coefficients	t	Collinearity Statistics	
	Beta		Tolerance	VIF
(Constant)		2.662		
5.A. Quantity of education	.298	4.997	.595	**1.681**
5.B. Quality of education	-.033	-.349	.236	**4.231**
5.C. On-the-job training	.686	7.821	.274	**3.646**

a. Dependent Variable: OVRL

The test of the existence of linear relationships for LPI and PISA, LPI and GCI's 5th pillar, LPI and IMD's pillar

Four multivariate statistics calculated to test the null hypothesis that the canonical correlations are zero that there are no linear relationships between LPI and PISA, and LPI and GCI's fifth pillar variables. Since p values are less than 0.05 in the Pillais (the Pillai's trace), Hotellings (the Hotelling-Lawley trace) and Wilks (the Wilks' lambda) tests, the null hypothesis is rejected. Therefore, the alternative hypothesis that there are linear relationships between LPI and PISA, and LPI and GCI's fifth pillar variables is accepted. The Roys (the Roy's greatest root) test behaves differently from the other three tests. In cases where the remaining three are not statistically significant and Roy's is statistically significant, the effect considered not to be statistically significant (See Table A8 and A9). For LPI and IMD's variables, Hotellings' p is below the 0.05 threshold, thus there is an existence of linear relationships (See Table A10).

Table A8. Between LPI and PISA. "Effect .. Within Cells" Regression. Multivariate Tests of Significance (S = 3, M = 1, N = 23)

Test Name	Value	Approx. F	Hypoth. DF	Error DF	Sig. of F
Pillais	0.85	3.27	18	150.00	0.00
Hotellings	1.53	3.95	18	140.00	0.00
Wilks	0.33	3.64	18	136.25	0.00
Roys	0.52	-	-	-	-

Table A9. Between LPI and GCI's fifth pillar. "Effect .. Within Cells" Regression. Multivariate Tests of Significance (S = 3, M = 1, N = 59)

Test Name	Value	Approx. F	Hypoth. DF	Error DF	Sig. of F
Pillais	0.90	8.74	18	366.00	0.00
Hotellings	3.14	20.73	18	356.00	0.00
Wilks	0.21	13.67	18	339.90	0.00
Roys	0.75	-	-	-	-

Table A10. Between LPI and IMD's pillar. "Effect .. Within Cells" Regression. Multivariate Tests of Significance (S = 6, M = 4 1/2, N = 2)

Test Name	Value	Approx. F	Hypoth. DF	Error DF	Sig. of F
Pillais	3.75	1.14	96	66.00	0.29
Hotellings	43.32	1.96	96	26.00	0.03
Wilks	0.00	1.56	96	40.81	0.06
Roys	0.97	-	-	-	-

Factor analysis of LPI and IMD's scores

Retrieval of IMD Factors:

Table A11. KMO and Bartlett's Test

Kaiser-Meyer-Olkin Measure of Sampling Adequacy.		.6
Bartlett's Test of Sphericity	Approx. Chi-Square	426.165
	df	120
	Sig.	.000

Table A12. Total variance explained. Extraction method: Principal Component Analysis.

Component	Rotation Sums of Squared Loadings		
	Total	% of Variance	Cumulative %
1	1.151	7.194	7.194
2	1.129	7.058	14.252
3	1.102	6.890	21.142
4	1.084	6.778	27.920
5	1.082	6.764	34.684
6	1.059	6.620	41.304
7	1.022	6.389	47.693
8	1.019	6.371	54.064
9	.981	6.129	60.194
10	.975	6.093	66.286
11	.950	5.937	72.223
12	.933	5.828	78.052
13	.899	5.616	83.668
14	.878	5.487	89.155
15	.870	5.437	94.592
16	.865	5.408	100

Extraction Method: Principal Component Analysis.

Table A13. Rotated component matrix[a]

Components:	1	2	3	4	5	6	7	8
84.Science in schools	0.885							
78.Student mobility inbound		0.93						
79.Student mobility outbound			0.972					
74.Pupil-teacher ratio (primary education)				0.916				
77.Higher education achievement (%					0.884			
75.Pupil-teacher ratio (secondary						0.874		
76.Secondary school enrollment (%)							0.793	
82.English proficiency - TOEFL								0.808
Components:	9	10	11	12	13	14	15	16
72.Total public expenditure on education	0.777							
88.Language skills		0.74						
81.Educational assessment Science			0.674					
80.Educational assessment Mathematics				0.662				
87.Illiteracy (%)					-0.73			
86.Management education						0.589		
83.Educational system							0.584	
85.University education								0.566

Extraction Method: Principal Component Analysis.
Rotation Method: Equamax with Kaiser Normalization.
a. Rotation converged in 61 iterations.

Retrieval of LPI Factors:

Table A14. KMO and Bartlett's Test

Kaiser-Meyer-Olkin Measure of Sampling Adequacy.		.934
Bartlett's Test of Sphericity	Approx. Chi-Square	600.078
	df	15
	Sig.	.000

Table A15. Total variance explained. Extraction method: Principal Component Analysis.

Component	Rotation Sums of Squared Loadings		
	Total	% of Variance	Cumulative %
1	1.050	17.492	17.492
2	1.028	17.129	34.621
3	.997	16.622	51.243
4	.988	16.473	67.716
5	.973	16.208	83.924
6	.965	16.076	100

Extraction Method: Principal Component Analysis.

Table A16. Rotated component matrix[a]

	1	2	3	4	5	6
TIME	.715					
ITRN		.683				
CUST			.630			
TRAC				.616		
INFR					.587	
LOGS						.576

Extraction Method: Principal Component Analysis.
Rotation Method: Equamax with Kaiser Normalization.
a. Rotation converged in 71 iterations.

Table A17. WEF: 'Twelve pillars of economic competitiveness'. Highlighted row variable is used.

1-'Basic requirements' Institutions
2- Infrastructure
3- Macroeconomic stability
4- Health and primary education
5-'Efficiency enhancers' Higher education and training
6-Goods market efficiency
7- Labour market efficiency
8- Financial market sophistication
9-Technological readiness
10-Market size 'Innovation and sophistication factors'
11-Business sophistication
12-Innovation

Table A18. IMD: Four categories with several sub-categories. Highlighted row variable is used.

Economic performance:
Domestic economy
International trade
International investment
Employment
Prices
Government efficiency:
Public Finance
Fiscal policy
Institutional framework
Business legislation
Societal framework
Business efficiency:
Productivity and efficiency
Labour market
Finance
Management practices
Attitudes and values
Infrastructure:
Basic infrastructure
Technological infrastructure
Scientific infrastructure
Health and environment
Education

Part IV
Transport Mode & Fuel Type

Chapter 5. The dynamic relationships between the choices of transport mode and fuel type: the case of Turkey

Abstract. The transport infrastructure has significant direct and indirect effects on productivity and economic growth because transportation costs influence to some degree the provision of the majority of goods and services. Continued economic growth in Turkey combined with rising urbanization has placed increasing demand on various modes of transportation. By using various data drawn from the World Bank database, this study applies time series analysis in order to investigate the dynamic relationship between the choices of transport mode and fuel type in Turkey. The results of the presented unit root tests and co-integration analyses indicate that high gasoline prices and thus increased demand for diesel and decreased gasoline consumption have significant effects on transportation mode choices. Dynamic relationships are also shown to exist between the choices of transport mode and fuel type.

Keywords: transport, logistics, vehicle type choice, fuel consumption, infrastructure, time series, vector autoregressive models, Granger causality

1. Introduction

The new millennium has thus far been characterized by continued growth in the demand for business and personal travel. Hence, transportation agencies and providers are striving to keep their assets in an acceptable condition in order to be able to provide the desired levels of service in the most cost-effective manner within the available resources (Sinha and Labi 2011).

The transportation system in many countries is typically the largest investment in the public sector (Sinha and Labi 2011), because transport has significant direct and indirect effects on national productivity and economic growth. The economic vitality and global competitiveness of a region or country are influenced by the quantity and quality of the prevailing transport infrastructure, as these facilities provide mobility and accessibility for people, goods, and services, and thereby play an important role in the economic production process (Sinha and Labi 2011). Indeed, it is widely argued that new transport infrastructure can significantly influence the local economy and the development potential of a region by providing increased accessibility and thus higher levels of efficiency and productivity (Banister 1995).

Location decisions and development are also strongly influenced by transport, and organizations often use transport data in order to make these decisions (Norwood and Casey 2002). In this regard, not only does transportation affect the economic conditions but the economic conditions also influence transportation (Norwood and Casey 2002). Governments, businesses, and individuals make investment decisions on the use of transportation on a daily basis (Norwood and Casey 2002). In addition, such relationships are constantly evolving owing to technological advancements, economic development, geographical changes, and many other factors (Norwood and Casey 2002).

Turkey, an upper-middle income country with a population of 73 million, has a diversified economy with a strategic geographical position, located on the southeast and southwest of Europe close to Asia. It is predominantly urban: the share of its urban population has grown by approximately a third to more than two-thirds since 1960, while per capita GDP has more than tripled during the same period to over US$10,000 (World Bank 2012).

Moreover, the urban population of Turkey is expected to increase by approximately 5 percent per decade until 2020 (World Bank 2012).

The Turkish economy has experienced rapid growth over the past decade despite the impact of the global economic crisis. Turkey's GDP increased by 7 percent per year during 2002–2008 and even though the global recession of 2008–2009 caused the economy to contract by 4.7 percent in 2009, Turkey recovered quickly thanks in part to a policy of monetary and fiscal expansion based on the strong capital buffers built up over the previous decade, and growth reached 8.9 percent in 2010 and 8 percent in 2011. In line with this strong economic growth, public spending on transport in Turkey has increased substantially in recent years. Public expenditure on transport almost doubled from 1.06 percent of GDP in 2004 to 1.92 percent in 2010, with the transport sector accounting for the bulk of the increase in total public investment during this period (World Bank 2012). The continued economic growth of Turkey combined with rapid urbanization, however, has placed increasing demand on various modes of transportation. Meeting this rising demand is therefore a priority for further economic development (World Bank 2012).

As in many developing countries, fuel prices in Turkey are increasing, rising from approximately 0.50 US$/liter in 1990 to 2.54 US$/liter in 2012. Tax on fuel is very high (approximately 75 percent), which contributes 10 percent of the national budget in Turkey. Additionally, taxes on road transport provide an average of 12 percent of the national budget. Therefore, the direct and indirect effects of oil shocks are negative and very large in Turkey. The indirect effects of spiraling oil prices and gas costs include rising imports of non-energy products (Aydin and Acar 2011). Indeed, the cost of fuel affects the prices of the majority of the other goods and services in the economy.

Based on the foregoing, the present study examines whether there is a dynamic relationship between the choices of transport mode and fuel type in Turkey. We aim to answer the following research questions: What are the causalities between passengers' transport modes and the choice of transferring goods? What is the influence of the reduction in gasoline consumption? Does the overall length of railway lines cause any increase in the number of railway passengers? Which modes of transportation does the increase in diesel consumption affect most?

This study applies time series analysis in order to explore the dynamic relationship between the choices of transport mode and fuel type in Turkey. Methodologically, unit root tests and co-integration analyses are conducted to investigate this dynamic relationship. Then, causality tests are performed to test the formulated hypotheses.

The remainder of this study is organized as follows. Section 2 reviews the literature. Section 3 describes the data and methods used for the analysis. Section 4 presents and discusses the research findings. The study is concluded in Section 5.

2. *Literature review*

There has long been an implicit assumption of a positive bidirectional link between transport and development (Banister 1995). According to Banister (1995), countries, regions, and cities that attract a high proportion of transport investment have a competitive advantage over places that are less successful at obtaining such investment. Underhill (2010) states that transportation-related infrastructure such as roads, bridges, tunnels, railways, canals, seaports, and airports is a cornerstone of modern economies. Transport has a major impact on the economic and spatial development of cities and regions, because the attractiveness of particular locations rests on their relative accessibility, which depends on the quality and quantity of the transport infrastructure (Banister 1995). However, while a high-quality transport infrastructure has long been considered to be a prerequisite for economic development, this hypothesis has never been studied in depth (Banister and Berechman 1999).

Norwood and Casey (2002) acknowledge that relationships between transport and the economy are complex and poorly understood. Transport is a massive undertaking that has significant direct and indirect effects on productivity and economic growth as well as being an enabler of international trade since physical movements precede financial transactions (Norwood and Casey 2002). These authors also state that governments, businesses, and individuals make investment decisions on transport and transit use on a daily basis and thus that location decisions and development are strongly influenced by transport.

Fuel economy is attracting the attention of policymakers in a way not seen for nearly two decades (National Research Council 2002). Concerns have grown over the reliability of the supply of gasoline, especially during the peak driving season, while evidence continues to accumulate that climate change should be taken seriously (National Research Council 2002). Because a safe, secure, clean, and affordable transport network is essential for social and economic vitality, there will be many serious challenges to energy systems and transportation that must be met over the next 50 years and beyond (National Research Council 2003). Population growth, economic growth, increasingly stringent environmental constraints such as the pressure to limit carbon dioxide emissions, and the geopolitical impacts on the availability of energy and the energy market are the driving forces in this regard. Science and technology, particularly chemistry and chemical engineering, will play a role in meeting these challenges (National Research Council 2003).

According to Banister and Berechman (1999), in developed countries where there is already a well-connected transport system, high investment in this infrastructure will not result in further economic growth. However, investment in transport infrastructure acts as a complement to other underlying conditions, which must also be satisfied if the pursuit of economic development is to be successful (Banister and Berechman 1999). Additional investment in transport, while not a necessary condition, therefore plays a supporting role when other factors are at work (Banister and Berechman 1999). In this vein, Martin (1999) finds that the direct effects of transport infrastructure are mainly the economic consequences of its construction, maintenance, and repair. Furthermore, in most EU countries, the economic importance of the transport sector is considerable and these effects may become even more important at the regional level (Martin 1999).

In recent years, a large number of empirical studies of the effects on the productivity of public investment have been carried out based on the work of Aschauer (1989), Munnell (1990), and Martin (1999). Aschauer (1989) argues that there is a causal link between the decline in U.S. investment in public infrastructure in the early 1970s and the resulting productivity slowdown. Although Aschauer estimates that the marginal product of public capital is very high (Martin 1999), other analysts criticize these approaches for methodological reasons. They argue, for example, that first differences rather than global values should be used for the specification of equations (Tatom 1991; Hulten and Schwab 1993). Tatom (1993), by using co-integration estimates, also fails to find a positive and significant link between infrastructure and growth.

Bhatnagar (2009) points out seven factors that affect transport mode selection. These are (1) the strengths and weaknesses of the company in terms of marketing, financial, and production resources, (2) the characteristics of the current market, including competitive scenario and geographical and territorial structure, (3) the equity necessary to support out of stocks, (4) product characteristics and the suitability of various modes of transport, (5) quantity to be carried, (6) distance, and (7) transport costs. Bhatnagar (2009) states that the higher the value of a product (such as electronics or pharmaceuticals), the more its transportation network should focus on responsiveness, while the lower the value of a product (e.g., bulk goods such as grain or wood), the more its network should focus on efficiency.

The literature on transportation and its choices is substantial, including studies in numerous fields such as Business and Economics, Engineering, Operations Research and Management Science, Transportation, Sciences and Ecology, Urban Studies, Environmental, and Public Administration. Some of the most recent publications on transportation, vehicle choices, and fuel types are presented in Table 1.

Table 1. Highlighted studies about transportation, vehicle choices, and fuel types.

Field of study	Authors
Business *and* Economics, Engineering, Operations Research *and* Management Science, Transportation, Sciences *and* Ecology, Urban Studies, Environmental, Public Administration	Bhat *et al.* (2009), Lee *et al.* (2003), Kim (2012), Lane (2012), Krutilla and Graham (2012), Brownstone and Golob (2009), Adjemian *et al.* (2010), Macharis *et al.* (2010), Rodier and Johnston (2002), Sandoval *et al.* (2009), Wang (2011), Watcharasukarn *et al.* (2012)
Engineering, Transportation, Telecommunications	Adjemian and Williams (2009), Farooq *et al.* (2012), Ferdous *et al.* (2010), Haire and Machemehl (2010), Hess *et al.* (2012), Holguin-Veras (2002), Mohammadian and Miller (2002), Osula and Adebisi (2001), Spissu *et al.* (2009), Zhang and Lu (2012), Lu *et al.* (2011), Pirdavani *et al.* (2013)
Environmental Sciences *and* Ecology, Transportation	Potoglou (2008), Potoglou and Kanaroglou (2008)
Public, Environmental *and* Occupational Health, Transportation	Wheatley and Di Stefano (2008)
Transportation	Andreoli *et al.* (2010), Cheaitou and Cariouz (2012), Khoo *et al.* (2012), Psaraftis and Kontovas (2013), Samimi *et al.* (2011)

3. Data and method

3.1 Data

The data on Turkey used in the presented time series analysis are derived from the World Bank database (see Figures 1 and 2).

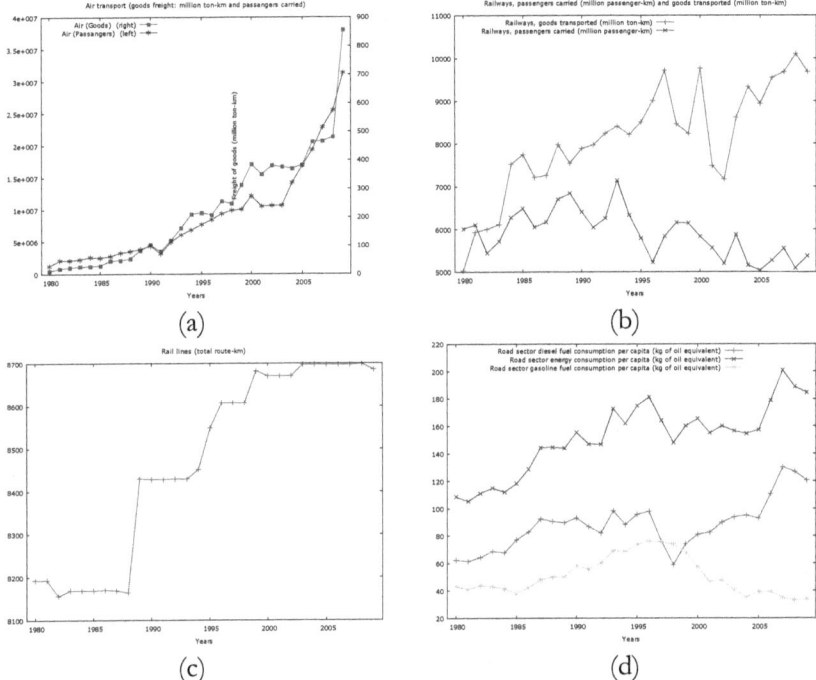

Figure 1. Time series data for Turkey. (a) Air transport, freight (million ton-km) and passengers carried, (b) Railways, goods transported (million ton-km) and passengers carried (million passenger-km), (c) Rail lines (total route-km), (d) Road sector energy consumption per capita (kg of oil equivalent), gasoline fuel consumption per capita (kg of oil equivalent) and diesel fuel consumption per capita (kg of oil equivalent)

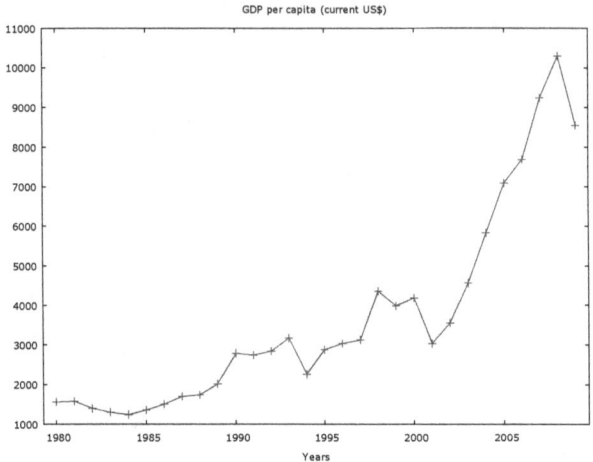

Figure 2. GDP per capita of Turkey (current US$)

3.2 Method

The analysis presented herein follows these main steps. First, unit root tests are conducted. Following these tests, diagnostic tests, the specification of lag length, and stability analyses are performed. Next, co-integration tests are conducted. Finally, causality tests are carried out.

3.2.1 Unit root tests

A univariate time series is said to have a unit root when one of the roots of the polynomial determinant series has a magnitude equal to 1 (on the unit circle). For a stationary series, all roots should lie outside the unit circle (implying parameters with magnitudes less than 1); explosive roots lie inside the unit circle. A stationary series has a definite expected value, or mean, and mean reversion, which means it tends to return to its central value. Nonstationary series (those with unit or explosive roots) do not have an unconditional expected value, but rather conditional expected values only for a specific period of time, conditioned by an initial condition. The statistical distributions of many estimators of sampling theory depend on the properties of the stationary time series being modeled. Therefore, the test series for unit (and explosive) roots have grown in importance during the past 15 years as the theory of the distribution of stationary and nonstationary series has been better understood and developed (Dorfman

1997).

The standard unit root test is the Dickey–Fuller test, which tests the null hypothesis of a unit root against the alternative of a stationary root (Dorfman 1997). Nonetheless, other tests have been developed that allow for heteroscedasticity (Phillips and Perron 1988) and unknown lag length (Dickey and Pantula 1987) as well as other parameterizations in terms of trend and drift, which are more stable under the assumptions both null and alternative hypotheses (Schmidt and Phillips 1992).

Because the order of integration of time series is of great importance for the analysis, several statistical tests were developed for the investigation. The augmented Dickey–Fuller test statistic (ADF) is based on the t-statistic of the coefficient estimated by using OLS (Luetkepohl et al. 2004). The ADF-GLS test is a variant of the Dickey–Fuller test for a unit root where the test statistic is assumed to have a mean of non-zero or show a linear trend. The difference is that the de-meaning or de-trending of the variables is carried out by using the GLS procedure suggested by Elliott et al. (1996). This method provides a test with a greater power than the standard Dickey–Fuller approach.

The KPSS test (Kwiatkowski et al. 1992), which is another possibility to investigate the properties of the integration of a series $y(t)$, aims to test the null hypothesis that the data generation process is stationary (H0: $y(t) \sim I(0)$) against the alternative that it is I(1) (H1: $y(t) \sim I(1)$). The KPSS test thus assesses the stationarity of the variable (or its first difference). The null hypothesis is that the variable in question is stationary, either around a level or, if the "include trend" is checked, around a linear deterministic trend. The selected lag order determines the size of the window used for Bartlett smoothing. The critical values given for the test statistic are based on the response surfaces estimated by Sephton (1995), which are more accurate for small samples than the values provided by Kwiatkowski et al. (1992). When the test statistic is between a 1 percent and 10 percent critical value, a p-value is shown, which is obtained through linear interpolation and should not be taken too literally.

Table 2 depicts the unit root tests for the variables in the present study. This test is important because if one or more of the variables has a unit root, there may be an error correction mechanism and the Granger causality tests may be suspect.

Table 2. Unit root tests – log levels (natural logarithm) and first differences

Variables/Tests	ADF-GLS H₀: Unit root H₁: Stationarity	KPSS H₀: Stationarity H₁: Unit root
Log levels		
l_[Air (goods)]	-2.212	0.143*
l_[Air (passengers)]	-3.010*	0.281***
l_[Diesel consumption (per capita)]	-2.796	0.128*
l_[Gasoline consumption (per capita)]	-2.000	0.138*
l_[Rail (goods)]	-1.449	0.146*
l_[Rail (passengers)]	-1.713	0.145*
l_[Rail total]	-2.718	0.133*
l_[Road energy consumption (per capita)]	-2.105	0.135*
l_[GDP (per capita)]	-2.651	0.181**
1st differences of log levels		
Δl_[Air (goods)]	-1.231***	0.278
Δl_[Air (passengers)]	-4.291***	0.246
Δl_[Diesel consumption (per capita)]	-4.955***	0.151
Δl_[Gasoline consumption (per capita)]	-2.012**	0.235
Δl_[Rail (goods)]	-6.100***	0.322
Δl_[Rail (passengers)]	-6.194***	0.191
Δl_[Rail total]	-1.206	0.171
Δl_[Road energy consumption (per capita)]	-5.046***	0.199
Δl_[GDP (per capita)]	-3.874***	0.284

***, **, and * denote the rejection of the null hypothesis of unit roots for the ADF-GLS test at the 1%, 5% and 10% significance levels.

***, **, and * denote the rejection of the null hypothesis of stationarity for the KPSS test at the 1%, 5% and 10% significance levels.

ADF-GLS: A variant of the augmented Dickey–Fuller test
KPSS: Kwiatkowski, Phillips, Schmidt, Shin stationarity test
H₀ : Null hypothesis, H₁: Alternative hypothesis

Initial analysis: Diagnostic tests of the residuals

The test case for residual autocorrelation verifies the null hypothesis that there is no remaining residual autocorrelation at lag 1 h against the other, namely at least one autocorrelation is non-zero (Luetkepohl *et al.* 2004). Ljung and Box (1978) propose a modified version of the statistical case for which the χ2 approximation is considered to be more appropriate in some situations (see Luetkepohl *et al.* 2004).

The LM test for residual autocorrelation in AR models is another test of residual autocorrelation, sometimes known as the Breusch–Godfrey test. This test is based on the examination of an AR (h) model for residues and the verification of the pair of hypotheses (Luetkepohl et al. 2004). The ARCH-LM test, which is a popular test for neglected conditional heteroscedasticity, is based on fitting an ARCH (q) model to estimate residues and test the null hypothesis (Luetkepohl et al. 2004). Based on the tests performed, we found that autocorrelation does not exist and that there is no ARCH effect (see Tables 3 and 4).

Table 3. Autocorrelation test

Variables	Equation num.	Ljung–Box Q'	P-value	Result at the 5% level
[Air (goods)] (t)	Equation 1	0.662323	0.416	Accept H₀
[Air (passengers)] (t)	Equation 2	2.02184	0.155	Accept H₀
[Rail total] (t)	Equation 3	0.180634	0.671	Accept H₀
[Rail (goods)] (t)	Equation 4	0.00385613	0.95	Accept H₀
[Rail (passengers)] (t)	Equation 5	0.135968	0.712	Accept H₀
[Diesel consumption (per capita)] (t)	Equation 6	0.297243	0.586	Accept H₀
[Road energy consumption (per capita)] (t)	Equation 7	0.514212	0.473	Accept H₀
[Gasoline consumption (per capita)] (t)	Equation 8	1.94356	0.163	Accept H₀
[GDP (per capita)] (t)	Equation 9	0.45371	0.501	Accept H₀

H₀: no autocorrelation is present

Table 4. Test for ARCH of order 1

Variables	Equation num.	LM test	p-value	Result at the 5% level
[Air (goods)] (t)	Equation 1	0.503031	0.478171	Accept H₀
[Air (passengers)] (t)	Equation 2	0.056781	0.811658	Accept H₀
[Rail total] (t)	Equation 3	2.08034	0.149206	Accept H₀
[Rail (goods)] (t)	Equation 4	0.0150115	0.902486	Accept H₀
[Rail (passengers)] (t)	Equation 5	0.261072	0.609384	Accept H₀
[Diesel consumption (per capita)] (t)	Equation 6	0.48424	0.486508	Accept H₀
[Road energy consumption (per capita)] (t)	Equation 7	0.122894	0.725917	Accept H₀
[Gasoline consumption (per capita)] (t)	Equation 8	2.72246	0.0989452	Accept H₀
[GDP (per capita)] (t)	Equation 9	0.0837748	0.772246	Accept H₀

H₀: no ARCH effect is present

Table 5 presents the Akaike information criterion (AIC), Bayesian information criterion (BIC), and Hannan–Quinn information criterion (HQC) values for VARs with 1 to 2 lags. These should be interpreted as fit statistics that describe the improvement in the log-likelihood, penalized for the additional lags. Smaller values of these fit statistics are better. Based on this table, one could choose a lag length of p=1. The asterisks below Table 5 indicate the best (minimized) values of the respective information criteria. The VAR(p) model is $z(t) = A(1)z(t-1) + ... + A(p)z(t-p) + B.d(t) + u(t)$, where d(t) is a vector of deterministic variables: d(t)= 1 and t (1980=1). For more details of the information criteria concepts refer to http://davegiles.blogspot.com.tr/2013/07/information-criteria-unveiled.html#more

Table 5. Information criteria (selected p is 1)

p	AIC	HQC	BIC
1*	-5.08391E+01*	-4.93772E+01*	-4.61714E+01*
2	0.00000E+00	0.00000E+00	0.00000E+00

$z(t,1)$ = L_[Air (goods)], $z(t,2)$ = L_[Air (passengers)], $z(t,3)$ = L_[Rail total)], $z(t,4)$ = L_[Rail (goods)], $z(t,5)$ = L_[Rail (passengers)], $z(t,6)$ = L_[Diesel consumption (per capita)], $z(t,7)$ = L_[Road energy consumption (per capita)], $z(t,8)$ = L_[Gasoline (per capita)], $z(t,9)$ = L_[GDP (per capita)]

Dependent variables: $Y(1)$ = L_[Air (goods)], $Y(2)$ = L_[Air (passengers)], $Y(3)$ = L_[Rail total)], $Y(4)$ = L_[Rail (goods)], $Y(5)$ = L_[Rail (passengers)], $Y(6)$ = L_[Diesel consumption (per capita)], $Y(7)$ = L_[Road energy consumption (per capita)], $Y(8)$ = L_[Gasoline (per capita)], $Y(9)$ = L_[GDP (per capita)]

The VAR lag length is typically specified by using a combination of statistical adjustments and test statistics for the length formal latency. It must be remembered, however, that any finite length offset order is only an approximation of the length (possibly) infinite lag order. Therefore, in applied work, it is necessary to adopt a holistic approach to search latency tests and fit statistics. In this analysis, a 1-lag VAR model is used. In each of nine variable control equations, an interception and trend are included.

VAR processes are a class of suitable model used to describe the data generation process of a small or medium set of time series variables. In these models, all variables are often treated as *a priori* endogenous, and they reflect the rich dynamics (Luetkepohl *et al.* 2004). A vector error correction model arises when several variables are driven by a common stochastic trend, as may occur in some series. In this case, they have a particularly strong link and thus may also be of interest from an economic standpoint. Following Granger (1981) and Engle and Granger (1987), the variables are co-integrated if they have a common stochastic trend. If such co-integrating relationships are present in a system of variables, the VAR form is not the most convenient configuration model. In this case, it is useful to examine specific parameterizations that support the analysis of the structure of co-integration (i.e., vector error correction models or vector equilibrium correction models) (Luetkepohl *et al.* 2004). The lag order selection test results are shown in Table 6.

Table 6. VAR system. Lag order 1 and includes trend and robust HC1:

VAR system, **lag order 1**
OLS estimates, observations 1981-2009 (T = 29)
Log-likelihood = 465.81755
Determinant of covariance matrix = 9.0337768e-026
AIC = -25.2978
BIC = -20.6301
HQC = -23.8359
Portmanteau test: LB(7) = 724.003, df = 486 [0.0000]

Stability analysis

Stability analysis is another important way in which to verify a model in order to examine its stability over time. For this purpose, estimates from different subperiods are generally calculated and examined. Chow tests provide a formal way to do this by allowing researchers to test conventional structural change. Variants such as split samples, breakpoint, and forecast tests are often reported (Luetkepohl *et al.* 2004).

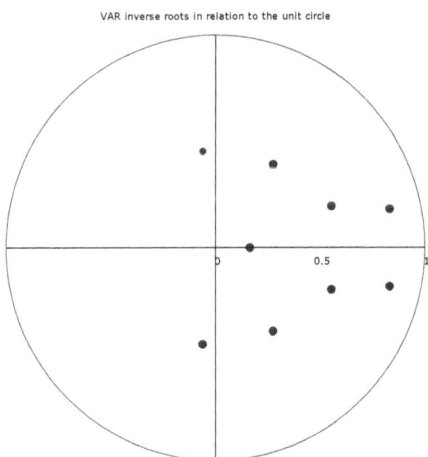

Figure 3. VAR inverse roots

The VAR model is dynamically stable. VAR inverse roots are inside the unit circle (see Figure 3). (For more details of the stability concept: http://davegiles.blogspot.ca/2013/06/when-is-autoregressive-model.html)

3.2.2 Co-integration test

Granger (1981) notes that vectors of variables that all achieve stationarity after differentiation may have linear combinations that are stationary in level (see Baltagi 2008). Later, Granger (1986) and Engle and Granger (1987) were the first to formalize the idea of integrated variables sharing an equilibrium relationship that turned out to be stationary or have a low degree of integration of the original series (see Baltagi 2008). They noted that property co-integration, which means co-movements between variables, could be exploited to test for the existence of equilibrium relationships within a fully dynamic specification (Baltagi 2008). For two or more unit root process, there may be fixed linear combinations that can be interpreted as long run relationships. This phenomenon is called co-integration (Baltagi 2008).

In the first row in Table 7, for a rank value of 0, the trace test value is 15.507 and the p value is 0.0626 ($p < 0.10$). Therefore, the null hypothesis of *"no long run relationship"* is rejected. In the second row, for a rank value of 1, the trace test value is 1.5761 and there exists co-integration of order 1 because the p value is 0.2334 ($p > 0.10$). Hence, the null hypothesis of the *"existence of co-integration of order 1"* is not rejected. Thus, the length of railways and number of railway passengers are co-integrated, namely they have a long run relationship (see Table 8).

Table 7. l_[Rail (total)] and l_[Rail (goods)] are co-integrated I(1):

Rank	Eigenvalue	Trace test	p-value	Lmax test	p-value
0	0.38144	15.507	0.0482	13.931	0.0546
1	0.052896	1.5761	0.2093	1.5761	0.2093

Log-likelihood = 222.681 (including constant term: 140.382)

Table 8. Corrected for sample size (df = 26)

Rank	Trace test	p-value
0	15.507	0.0626
1	1.5761	0.2334

3.2.3 Causality test

The concept of causality introduced by Granger (1969) is perhaps the most widely discussed in the econometrics literature. Granger defines a variable y_{1t} as causal for another time series variable y_{2t} if the former helps predict the latter (see Baltagi 2008). Table 9 presents the results of the F tests from the VAR for Granger causality.

Table 9. Hypotheses tests for Granger causality

Null hypothesis (H_0)	F-Statistic	Prob.	Result
Rail (passengers) *does not Granger cause* Air (goods)	5.0455	0.0375**	Reject H_0
Gasoline consumption (per capita) *does not Granger cause* Air (goods)	6.0372	0.0244**	Reject H_0
Gasoline consumption (per capita) *does not Granger cause* Air (passengers)	4.0497	0.0594***	Reject H_0
Air (goods) *does not Granger cause* Rail (goods)	3.7436	0.0689***	Reject H_0
Diesel consumption (per capita) *does not Granger cause* Rail (goods)	7.334	0.0144**	Reject H_0
Road energy consumption (per capita) *does not Granger cause* Rail (goods)	4.3867	0.0506***	Reject H_0
Gasoline consumption (per capita) *does not Granger cause* Rail (goods)	7.0138	0.0163**	Reject H_0
Rail (total) *does not Granger cause* Rail (passengers)	3.5463	0.0759***	Reject H_0
Road energy consumption (per capita) *does not Granger cause* Diesel consumption (per capita)	3.7627	0.0682***	Reject H_0
Diesel consumption (per capita) *does not Granger cause* Road energy consumption (per capita)	6.2886	0.0220**	Reject H_0
Gasoline consumption (per capita) *does not Granger cause* Road energy consumption (per capita)	5.3675	0.0325**	Reject H_0
Rail (total) *does not Granger cause* Diesel consumption (per capita)	5.9919	0.0249**	Reject H_0

*** and ** denote rejection of the null hypothesis at the 10% and 5% significance levels.

All null hypotheses are rejected based on the Granger causality test results above. Therefore, it is safe to accept the alternative hypotheses for the causality tests. For more details, see Appendix section.

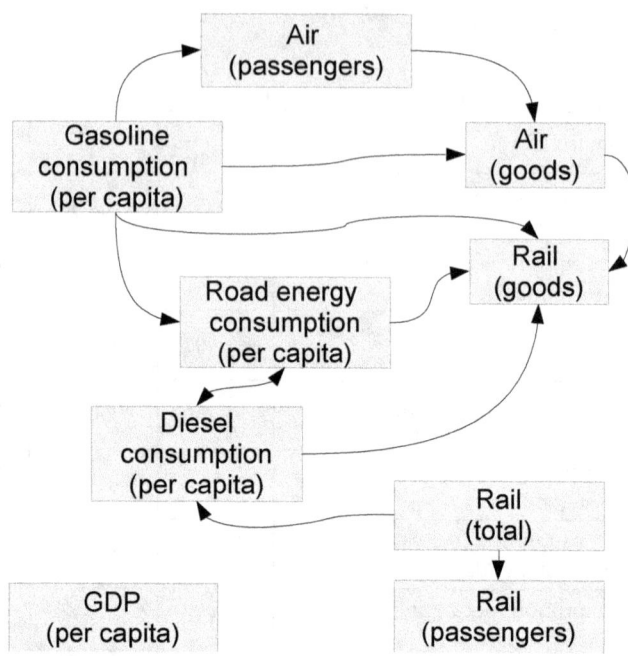

Figure 4. Variables and directions of Granger causalities

Figure 4 shows the direction of causalities. In summary, (1) rail (passengers) causes air (goods), (2) gasoline consumption (per capita) causes air (goods), (3) gasoline consumption (per capita) causes air (passengers), (4) air (goods) causes rail (goods), (5) diesel consumption (per capita) causes rail (goods), (6) road energy consumption (per capita) causes rail (goods), (7) gasoline consumption (per capita) causes rail (goods), (8) rail (total) causes rail (passengers), (9) road energy consumption (per capita) causes diesel consumption (per capita), (10) diesel consumption (per capita) causes road energy consumption (per capita), (11) gasoline consumption (per capita) causes road energy consumption (per capita), and finally (12) rail (total) causes diesel consumption (per capita).

4. Findings and discussion

The analysis presented herein indicates that dynamic and significant relationships exist among the choices of transportation modes and fuel types. In particular, we find that increasing gasoline prices and thus increasing demand for diesel fuel and the decreasing trend of gasoline consumption per capita have significant positive effects on the number of airline passengers in addition to the goods transported by airlines and railways. Further, the increase in the length of railways positively affects the number of railway passengers carried and thereby diesel consumption per capita. However, rising GDP per capita has no significant effect on the choice of transportation mode, type of fuel consumption, or road energy consumption per capita (see Figure 4).

As productivity increases and becomes more efficient, its linear relationship with GDP may reduce because there is no a priori reason that transport demand is expected to increase with GDP (Banister and Berechman 1999). Moreover, production and distribution processes (e.g., the transport of passengers) could become less transport-intensive (Banister and Berechman 1999). Conversely, if prices rise significantly or there is concerted action at the international level, this simple linear relationship can be broken (Banister and Berechman 1999). For example, higher energy prices and greater production and consumption efficiency have resulted in a much lower GDP growth rate (Banister and Berechman 1999).

Further rises in transportation costs are expected over the next decade, with these increases anticipated to reach 4–5 percent of GDP, which is higher than that of average middle-income countries (World Bank 2012). The government's plans include tripling Turkey's road network from 2250 km to 7500 km by 2023, the construction of more than 12,000 km of new dual roads, and doubling the existing rail network to more than 25,000 km. The Turkish government also aims to provide a modal shift from road to rail, mainly due to its planned investments in a high speed rail network (up to 10,000 km of railways) (World Bank 2012).

Compared with other middle-income countries, Turkey's transport and logistics performance and its transport infrastructure (see Table 10) are average. The World Bank's Logistics Performance Index of 2011 ranks Turkey 39th of 155 countries, while the economic competitiveness of its transport infrastructure is better than Russia, Poland, and Brazil, and only moderately below the EU average. However, modes of transport, notably railways and seaports, are considered to be a greater obstacle to competitiveness and the environment by companies according to the World Bank's Enterprise Performance Survey (2008), with approximately half of exporting firms in Turkey seeing poor transportation as a barrier to business.

Table 10. Transportation infrastructure scores.

Countries / Economies	Airports	Ports	Railroads	Roads	Overall infrastructure
Turkey	5.4	4.1	2.7	4.7	5.1
OECD	5.6	5.2	4.5	5.1	5.5
EU-27	5.3	5.1	4.4	4.7	5.2
Top 10 Exporters	5.8	5.7	5.6	5.6	5.7

Source: World Economic Forum (2010/2011), World Competitiveness Report

Turkey, as an oil-importing developing economy, can also reduce the negative impact of oil price shocks if it were to diversify into non-oil energy sources. Common alternatives are renewable energy sources such as hydro, geothermal, solar, wind, and biofuels, which are substitutes for conventional transportation fuels (Aydin and Acar 2011). Designing efficient and cost-effective transportation systems that meet the prevailing environmental conditions is a major challenge, however (Haldenbilen 2006). Owing to limited natural resources and the world's current large-scale energy demands, modeling is becoming increasingly important to understand the mechanisms that degrade energy and resources and to develop systematic approaches that can improve systems and reduce the impact on the environment (Haldenbilen 2006). Nevertheless, the analysis of transportation in Turkey indicates potential efficiency gains in three main dimensions: (i) the modal split of investments, (ii) expenditure and efficiency resource management by public transport companies, and (iii) risk sharing through private sector funding (World Bank 2012).

The world is accelerating to over two billion vehicles, and we cannot deny that cars and trucks are an integral part of our lifestyle and our economy (Sperling et al. 2009). Cars provide mobility and personal freedom, while trucks transport goods that keep our economy humming (Sperling et al. 2009). Nevertheless, all these vehicles and our almost total dependence on gasoline to power them contribute to global warming and deplete the world's scarce natural resources (Sperling et al. 2009).

A number of factors have combined to place pressure on the price of gasoline, including increased global demand for crude oil and the limited refining capacity of gasoline suppliers (Vestus 2009). We cannot build a system of long-term transport based on the short-term availability of fuels (Chiras 2010). To ensure economic stability, we need a fuel that we can rely on (Chiras 2010). Building a transportation system based on fuel that will disappear in the near future is thus a valuable waste of energy, resources and time (Chiras 2010).

The road to survive and thrive is paved with vehicles that sip fuel and have low carbon emissions as well as electric vehicles, new mobility options and smart governance (Sperling *et al.* 2009). Informed consumers, policymakers and innovative firms around the world can lead us towards a sustainable future (Sperling *et al.* 2009). Global climate change, dependence on declining oil reserves and high fuel prices should be enough to convince humankind to create a lean green mode of transportation (Chiras 2010).

5. Conclusion

The transport infrastructure has significant direct and indirect effects on productivity and economic growth because transportation cost influences to some degree the provision of the majority of goods and services. Dynamic relationships exist between the choices of transport mode and fuel type. In particular, increasing gasoline prices and thus increasing demand for diesel fuel and the decreasing trend of gasoline consumption per capita has significant positive effects on the number of airline passengers as well as on those goods transported by airlines and railways. Further, increased railway infrastructure positively affects the number of railway passengers carried and diesel consumption per capita, but rising GDP per capita does not significantly affect transportation mode choice, type of fuel consumption, or road energy consumption per capita.

From a global perspective, it should be noted that increases in fuel prices and thus changing preferences towards transportation modes are not a country-specific issue. In addition, price increases affect industries, production, transport, agriculture and so on. High prices contribute to the slowdown of economic growth and may trigger inflation. Increased global demand for oil and the limited supply of this energy have already forced policymakers to consider alternatives. However, the sustainability of these alternative energy sources should also be examined. For instance, electric vehicles are putting increasing demand on rare earth elements such as magnets, which are used in electric engines. Additionally, the batteries used in these vehicles place rising demand on lithium and other elements, which are not abundant. In other words, the sustainable alternatives are not cheap, and they might not become any cheaper in the future. From the perspective of transportation issues, further research ought to be conducted on the sustainability of alternative modes by taking into consideration the limited supplies of rare earth elements and the way in which people live and consume on this fragile earth.

6. References

Adjemian, M. K., Lin, C. Y. C., & Williams, J. (2010). Estimating spatial interdependence in automobile type choice with survey data. *Transportation Research Part A-Policy and Practice*, 44(9), 661-675. doi: 10.1016/j.tra.2010.06.001

Adjemian, M., & Williams, J. (2009). Using census aggregates to proxy for household characteristics: an application to vehicle ownership. *Transportation*, 36(2), 223-241. doi: 10.1007/s11116-009-9191-2

Andreoli, D., Goodchild, A., & Vitasek, K. (2010). The rise of mega distribution centers and the impact on logistical uncertainty. *Transportation Letters-The International Journal of Transportation Research*, 2(2), 75-88. doi: 10.3328/tl.2010.02.02.75-88

Aschauer, D.A. (1989). Is public expenditure productive? *Journal of Monetary Economics*, 23(2), pp. 177–200.

Aydin, L., Acar, M. (2011). Economic impact of oil price shocks on the Turkish economy in the coming decades: A dynamic CGE analysis. *Energy Policy*, 39(3), 1722-1731.

Baltagi, B. H. (Editor). (2008). Companion to Theoretical Econometrics. Chichester, England: Wiley, pp. 611-691.

Banister, D. (1995). *Transport and Urban Development*. London, GBR: Spon Press, pp. 12-289.

Banister, D., Berechman, J. (1999). *Transport Investment and Economic Development*. London, GBR: Routledge, p 14.

Bhat, C. R., Sen, S., & Eluru, N. (2009). The impact of demographics, built environment attributes, vehicle characteristics, and gasoline prices on household vehicle holdings and use. *Transportation Research Part B-Methodological*, 43(1), 1-18. doi: 10.1016/j.trb.2008.06.009

Bhatnagar, A. (2009). Textbook of Supply Chain Management. Lucknow, IND: Global Media. p 138.

Brownstone, D., & Golob, T. F. (2009). The impact of residential density on vehicle usage and energy consumption. *Journal of Urban Economics*, 65(1), 91-98. doi: 10.1016/j.jue.2008.09.002

Cheaitou, A., & Cariouz, P. (2012). Liner shipping service optimisation with reefer containers capacity: an application to northern Europe-South America trade. *Maritime Policy and Management*, 39(6), 589-602. doi: 10.1080/03088839.2012.728726

Chiras, D. (2010). *Green Transportation Basics: A Green Energy Guide*. New York, NY, USA: New Society Publishers, 2010. p 8-11.

Dickey, D. A., & Pantula, S. G. (1987). Determining the order of differencing in autoregressive processes. *Journal of Business & Economic Statistics*, 5(4), 455-461. doi: 10.2307/1391997

Dorfman, J. H. (1997). *Bayesian Economics through Numerical Methods: A Guide to Econometrics and Decision Making with Prior Information*. Secaucus, NJ, USA: Springer, p 50.

Elliott, G., T.J. Rothenberg, & J.H. Stock (1996). Efficient tests for an autoregressive unit root. *Econometrica* 64, 813-836

Engle, R.F., Granger, C.W.J. (1987). Cointegration and Error Correction: Representation, Estimation and Testing, *Econometrica*, 55, 251-76.

Farooq, U., Siddiqui, M. A., Gao, L., & Hardy, J. L. (2012). Intelligent transportation systems: an impact analysis for Michigan. *Journal of Advanced Transportation*, 46(1), 12-25. doi: 10.1002/atr.138

Ferdous, N., Pinjari, A. R., Bhat, C. R., & Pendyala, R. M. (2010). A comprehensive analysis of household transportation expenditures relative to other goods and services: an application to United States consumer expenditure data. *Transportation*, 37(3), 363-390. doi: 10.1007/s11116-010-9264-2

Fuller, W.A. (1996). *Introduction to Statistical Time Series (2nd Ed.)*. New York: John Wiley

Granger, C. W. J. (1969). Investigating Causal Relations by Econometric Models and Cross-spectral Methods. *Econometrica* 37 (3): 424–438.

Granger, C.W.J. (1981). Some Properties of Time Series Data and Their Use in Econometric Model Specification, *Journal of Econometrics*, 16, 121-30.

Haire, A. R., & Machemehl, R. B. (2010). Regional and Modal Variability in Effects of Gasoline Prices on US Transit Ridership. *Transportation Research Record* (2144), 20-27. doi: 10.3141/2144-03

Haldenbilen, S. (2006). Fuel price determination in transportation sector using predicted energy and transport demand. *Energy Policy*, 34(17), 3078-3086.

Hess, S., Fowler, M., Adler, T., & Bahreinian, A. (2012). A joint model for vehicle type and fuel type choice: evidence from a cross-nested logit study. *Transportation*, 39(3), 593-625. doi: 10.1007/s11116-011-9366-5

Holguin-Veras, J. (2002). Revealed preference analysis of commercial vehicle choice process. *Journal of Transportation Engineering-ASCE*, 128(4), 336-346. doi: 10.1061/(asce)0733-947x(2002)128:4(336)

Hulten, C. R., & Schwab, R. M. (1993). *Endogenous Growth, Public Capital and the Convergence of Regional Manufacturing Industries*, Working Paper 4538, Cambridge, Mass.: NBER

Khoo, H. L., Ong, G. P., & Khoo, W. C. (2012). Short-term impact analysis of fuel price policy change on travel demand in Malaysian cities. *Transportation Planning and Technology*, 35(7), 715-736. doi: 10.1080/03081060.2012.710039

Kim, J. (2012). Endogenous vehicle-type choices in a monocentric city. *Regional Science and Urban Economics*, 42(4), 749-760. doi: 10.1016/j.regsciurbeco.2012.05.005

Krutilla, K., & Graham, J. D. (2012). Are Green Vehicles Worth the Extra Cost? The Case of Diesel-Electric Hybrid Technology for Urban Delivery Vehicles. *Journal of Policy Analysis and Management*, 31(3), 501-532. doi: 10.1002/pam.21641

Kwiatkowski, D., Phillips P., Schmidt P., & Shin Y. (1992). Testing the Null of Stationarity Against the Alternative of a Unit Root. *Journal of Econometrics*, 54, 159-178.

Lane, B. W. (2012). A time-series analysis of gasoline prices and public transportation in US metropolitan areas. *Journal of Transport Geography*, 22, 221-235. doi: 10.1016/j.jtrangeo.2011.10.006

Lee, S., Lee, Y. H., Park, J. H., Trb, & Trb. (2003). Estimating price and service elasticity of urban transportation demand with stated preference technique - Case in Korea Transportation Finance, *Economics and Economic Development 2003: Planning and Administration* (pp. 167-172).

Ljung, G.M., Box, G.E.P. (1978). On a Measure of a Lack of Fit in Time Series Models. *Biometrika* 65 (2): 297–303.

Lu, S. F., Hillmansen, S., Roberts, C. (2011). A Power-Management Strategy for Multiple-Unit Railroad Vehicles. *IEEE Transactions on Vehicular Technology*, 60(2), 406-420. doi: 10.1109/tvt.2010.2093911

Luetkepohl, H. (Editor), Kraetzig, M. (Editor), Phillips, P. C. B. (Contribution by). (2004). *Applied Time Series Econometrics*. West Nyack, NY, USA: Cambridge University Press, pp 11-87.

Macharis, C., Van Hoeck, E., Pekin, E., & van Lier, T. (2010). A decision analysis framework for intermodal transport: Comparing fuel price increases and the internalisation of external costs. *Transportation Research*

Part A-Policy and Practice, 44(7), 550-561. doi: 10.1016/j.tra.2010.04.006

Martin, R. (1999). *Regional Dimension in European Public Policy: Convergence or Divergence?* New York, NY USA: Palgrave Macmillan, p 143.

Mohammadian, A., Miller, E. J., & Trb. (2002). *Nested logit models and artificial neural networks for predicting household automobile choices - Comparison of performance Traveler Behavior and Values 2002: Planning and Administration* (pp. 92-100).

Munnell, A. (1990). Why has productivity growth declined? Productivity and public investment. *New England Economic Review*, January/February, pp. 4– 22.

National Research Council. (2002). Committee on the Effectiveness and Impact of Corporate Average Fuel Economy CAFE Standards Staff (Contribution by); National Research Council, Board on Energy and Environmental Systems Staff (Contribution by); National Research Council, Transportation Research Board Staff (Contribution by). *Effectiveness and Impact of Corporate Average Fuel Economy (CAFE) Standards*. Washington, DC, USA: National Academies Press, pp 7-9.

National Research Council. (2003). *Energy and Transportation: Challenges for the Chemical Sciences in the 21st Century*. Washington, DC, USA: National Academies Press, p 11.

Norwood, J. (Editor), Casey, J. (Editor), National Research Council Staff. (2002). *Key Transportation Indicators: Summary of a Workshop*. Washington, DC, USA: National Academies Press, p 22.

Osula, D. O. A., & Adebisi, O. (2001). Effects of fuel price increase in nigeria on travel expenditures. *Journal of Transportation Engineering-ASCE*, 127(2), 167-174. doi: 10.1061/(asce)0733-947x(2001)127:2(167)

Phillips, P.C.B., Perron, P. (1988): Testing for a Unit Root in Time Series Regression. *Biometrica*, 75, 335-346

Pirdavani, A., Brijs, T., Bellemans, T., Kochan, B., & Wets, G. (2013). Evaluating the road safety effects of a fuel cost increase measure by means of zonal crash prediction modeling. *Accident Analysis and Prevention*, 50, 186-195. doi: 10.1016/j.aap.2012.04.008

Potoglou, D. (2008). Vehicle-type choice and neighbourhood characteristics: An empirical study of Hamilton, Canada. *Transportation Research Part D-Transport and Environment*, 13(3), 177-186. doi: 10.1016/j.trd.2008.02.002

Potoglou, D., Kanaroglou, P. S. (2008). Disaggregate Demand Analyses for

Conventional and Alternative Fueled Automobiles: A Review. *International Journal of Sustainable Transportation*, 2(4), 234-259. doi: 10.1080/15568310701230398

Psaraftis, H. N., Kontovas, C. A. (2013). Speed models for energy-efficient maritime transportation: A taxonomy and survey. *Transportation Research Part C-Emerging Technologies*, 26, 331-351. doi: 10.1016/j.trc.2012.09.012

Rodier, C. J., Johnston, R. A. (2002). Uncertain socioeconomic projections used in travel demand and emissions models: could plausible errors result in air quality nonconformity? *Transportation Research Part A-Policy and Practice*, 36(7), 613-631. doi: 10.1016/s0965-8564(01)00026-x

Said, S.E. (1991). Unit Root Test for Time Series Data with a Linear Time Trend. *Journal of Econometrics*, 47, 285-303

Said, S.E., & Dickey, D. A. (1984). Testing for Unit Roots in Autoregressive Moving Average of Unknown Order. *Biometrika*, 71, 599-607

Samimi, A., Kawamura, K., Mohammadian, A. (2011). A behavioral analysis of freight mode choice decisions. *Transportation Planning and Technology*, 34(8), 857-869. doi: 10.1080/03081060.2011.600092

Sandoval, R., Karplus, V. J., Paltsev, S., Reilly, J. M. (2009). Modelling Prospects for Hydrogen-powered Transportation Until 2100. *Journal of Transport Economics and Policy*, 43, 291-316.

Sephton, P. S., 1995. Response surface estimates of the KPSS stationarity test, *Economics Letters*, Elsevier, vol. 47(3-4), pages 255-261, March.

Schmidt, P., Phillips, P. C. B. (1992). Lm tests for a unit-root in the presence of deterministic trends. *Oxford Bulletin of Economics and Statistics*, 54(3), 257-287. doi: 10.1111/j.1468-0084.1992.tb00002.x

Sinha, K. C., Labi, S. (2011). *Transportation Decision Making: Principles of Project Evaluation and Programming*. Hoboken, NJ, USA: Wiley, p 1.

Sperling, D., Gordon, D., Schwarzenegger, A. (Foreword by). (2009). Two Billion Cars: Driving Toward Sustainability. Cary, NC, USA: Oxford University Press, USA, 2009. p 8-277

Spissu, E., Pinjari, A. R., Pendyala, R. M., Bhat, C. R. (2009). A copula-based joint multinomial discrete-continuous model of vehicle type choice and miles of travel. *Transportation*, 36(4), 403-422. doi: 10.1007/s11116-009-9208-x

Tatom, J.A. (1991). Public capital and private sector performance. *Review (Federal Reserve Bank of St. Louis)*, 73, May/June, pp. 3–15.

Tatom, J. A. (1993). Paved with Good Intentions: the Mythical National

Infrastructure Crisis, Policy Analysis, Cato Institute, 12 August

Underhill, M. D., (2010). *Wiley Finance: Handbook of Infrastructure Investing.* Hoboken, NJ, USA: Wiley, p 19.

Vestus, W. P. (2009). *Fuel Prices: Rhyme or Reason?.* New York, NY, USA: Nova Science Publishers, Inc., 2009. p 15-79.

Wang, R. (2011). Shaping carpool policies under rapid motorization: the case of Chinese cities. *Transport Policy*, 18(4), 631-635. doi: 10.1016/j.tranpol.2011.03.005

Watcharasukarn, M., Page, S., Krumdieck, S. (2012). Virtual reality simulation game approach to investigate transport adaptive capacity for peak oil planning. *Transportation Research Part A-Policy and Practice*, 46(2), 348-367. doi: 10.1016/j.tra.2011.10.003

Wheatley, C. J., Di Stefano, M. (2008). Individualized Assessment of Driving Fitness for Older Individuals with Health, Disability, and Age-Related Concerns. *Traffic Injury Prevention*, 9(4), 320-327. doi: 10.1080/15389580801895269

World Bank. (2012). *Turkey - Transport Sector Expenditure Review: Synthesis Report.* © Washington, DC. https://openknowledge.worldbank.org /handle/10986/12307 License: CC BY 3.0 Unported.

World Economic Forum (2010). *World Competitiveness Report*

World Economic Forum (2011). *World Competitiveness Report*

Zhang, L., Lu, Y. J. (2012). Marginal-Cost Vehicle Mileage Fee. *Transportation Research Record* (2297), 1-10. doi: 10.3141/2297-01

Appendix

***, **, and * denote the significant values at the 1%, 5% and 10% significance levels.
For observations 1981-2009 (t):
Equation 1: [Air (goods)] (t)
Equation 2: [Air (passengers)] (t)
Equation 3: [Rail total] (t)
Equation 4: [Rail (goods)] (t)
Equation 5: [Rail (passengers)] (t)
Equation 6: [Diesel consumption (per capita)] (t)
Equation 7: [Road energy consumption (per capita)] (t)
Equation 8: [Gasoline consumption (per capita)] (t)
Equation 9: [GDP (per capita)] (t)

Table A1. Equation 1: log[Air (goods)] - Heteroskedasticity-robust standard errors

	Coefficient	Std. Error	t-ratio	p-value	
const	9.30074	49.5707	0.1876	0.85327	
log[Air (goods)]	-0.0134772	0.306474	-0.0440	0.96541	
log[Air (passengers)]	0.0772835	0.293747	0.2631	0.79546	
log[Rail total]	-1.72424	5.1349	-0.3358	0.74091	
log[Rail (goods)]	-0.13742	0.323187	-0.4252	0.67573	
log[Rail (passengers)]	1.04322	0.464431	2.2462	0.03748	**
log[Diesel consumption (per capita)]	1.13064	0.782921	1.4441	0.16588	
log[Road energy consumption (per capita)]	-2.05596	1.64489	-1.2499	0.22734	
log[Gasoline consumption (per capita)]	1.33814	0.544609	2.4571	0.02438	**
log[GDP (per capita)]	-0.0252117	0.270014	-0.0934	0.92664	
time	0.158314	0.0495022	3.1981	0.00498	***

Table A2. Descriptive statistics of Equation 1

Mean dependent var	4.977857	S.D. dependent var	1.120410
Sum squared resid	0.478795	S.E. of regression	0.163094
R-squared	0.986378	Adjusted R-squared	0.978810
F(10, 18)	308.6452	P-value(F)	5.19e-18
rho	-0.187944	Durbin-Watson	2.050422

Table A3. F-tests of zero restrictions of Equation 1

All lags of log[Air (goods)]	$F(1, 18) = 0.0019338\ [0.9654]$
All lags of log[Air (passengers)]	$F(1, 18) = 0.069219\ [0.7955]$
All lags of log[Rail total]	$F(1, 18) = 0.11275\ [0.7409]$
All lags of log[Rail (goods)]	$F(1, 18) = 0.1808\ [0.6757]$
All lags of log[Rail (passengers)]	$F(1, 18) = 5.0455\ [0.0375]$
All lags of log[Diesel consumption (per capita)]	$F(1, 18) = 2.0855\ [0.1659]$
All lags of log[Road energy consumption (per capita)]	$F(1, 18) = 1.5623\ [0.2273]$
All lags of log[Gasoline consumption (per capita)]	$F(1, 18) = 6.0372\ [0.0244]$
All lags of log[GDP (per capita)]	$F(1, 18) = 0.0087183\ [0.9266]$

Table A4. Equation 2: log[Air (passengers)] - Heteroskedasticity-robust standard errors

	Coefficient	Std. Error	t-ratio	p-value	
const	12.9472	41.6535	0.3108	0.75950	
log[Air (goods)]	-0.493094	0.318314	-1.5491	0.13877	
log[Air (passengers)]	0.516533	0.211492	2.4423	0.02514	**
log[Rail total]	-0.657865	4.31529	-0.1524	0.88053	
log[Rail (goods)]	-0.119476	0.303774	-0.3933	0.69871	
log[Rail (passengers)]	0.154506	0.337034	0.4584	0.65213	
log[Diesel consumption (per capita)]	0.809059	0.478582	1.6905	0.10817	
log[Road energy consumption (per capita)]	-1.30463	0.949064	-1.3746	0.18611	
log[Gasoline consumption (per capita)]	0.846317	0.420556	2.0124	0.05939	*
log[GDP (per capita)]	0.052619	0.232627	0.2262	0.82360	
time	0.123853	0.0558746	2.2166	0.03977	**

Table A5. Descriptive statistics of Equation 2

Mean dependent var	15.73824	S.D. dependent var	0.812735
Sum squared resid	0.277566	S.E. of regression	0.124179
R-squared	0.984992	Adjusted R-squared	0.976655
F(10, 18)	420.8046	P-value(F)	3.25e-19
rho	-0.254881	Durbin-Watson	2.477674

Table A6. F-tests of zero restrictions of Equation 2

All lags of log[Air (goods)]	$F(1, 18) = 2.3996\ [0.1388]$
All lags of log[Air (passengers)]	$F(1, 18) = 5.965\ [0.0251]$
All lags of log[Rail total]	$F(1, 18) = 0.023241\ [0.8805]$
All lags of log[Rail (goods)]	$F(1, 18) = 0.15469\ [0.6987]$
All lags of log[Rail (passengers)]	$F(1, 18) = 0.21016\ [0.6521]$
All lags of log[Diesel consumption (per capita)]	$F(1, 18) = 2.8579\ [0.1082]$
All lags of log[Road energy consumption (per capita)]	$F(1, 18) = 1.8896\ [0.1861]$
All lags of log[Gasoline consumption (per capita)]	$F(1, 18) = 4.0497\ [0.0594]$
All lags of log[GDP (per capita)]	$F(1, 18) = 0.051164\ [0.8236]$

Table A7. Equation 3: log[Rail total] - Heteroskedasticity-robust standard errors

	Coefficient	Std. Error	t-ratio	p-value
const	5.07183	2.93041	1.7308	0.10060
log[Air (goods)]	-0.00842692	0.00979278	-0.8605	0.40082
log[Air (passengers)]	0.000987149	0.00679314	0.1453	0.88608
log[Rail total]	0.425746	0.329772	1.2910	0.21303
log[Rail (goods)]	-0.0128719	0.0109624	-1.1742	0.25562
log[Rail (passengers)]	0.0231871	0.0211354	1.0971	0.28707
log[Diesel consumption (per capita)]	0.00858873	0.0226056	0.3799	0.70844
log[Road energy consumption (per capita)]	-0.019481	0.0445654	-0.4371	0.66721
log[Gasoline consumption (per capita)]	0.0282305	0.0166629	1.6942	0.10746
log[GDP (per capita)]	-0.00581176	0.00664911	-0.8741	0.39360
time	0.00362771	0.0022652	1.6015	0.12667

Table A8. Descriptive statistics of Equation 3

Mean dependent var	9.045043	S.D. dependent var	0.025697
Sum squared resid	0.000634	S.E. of regression	0.005933
R-squared	0.965732	Adjusted R-squared	0.946694
$F(10, 18)$	239.1882	P-value(F)	5.04e-17
rho	-0.075239	Durbin-Watson	2.142907

Table A9. F-tests of zero restrictions of Equation 3

All lags of log[Air (goods)]	$F(1, 18) =$ 0.7405 [0.4008]
All lags of log[Air (passengers)]	$F(1, 18) =$ 0.021117 [0.8861]
All lags of log[Rail total]	$F(1, 18) =$ 1.6668 [0.2130]
All lags of log[Rail (goods)]	$F(1, 18) =$ 1.3787 [0.2556]
All lags of log[Rail (passengers)]	$F(1, 18) =$ 1.2036 [0.2871]
All lags of log[Diesel consumption (per capita)]	$F(1, 18) =$ 0.14435 [0.7084]
All lags of log[Road energy consumption (per capita)]	$F(1, 18) =$ 0.19109 [0.6672]
All lags of log[Gasoline consumption (per capita)]	$F(1, 18) =$ 2.8704 [0.1075]
All lags of log[GDP (per capita)]	$F(1, 18) =$ 0.76399 [0.3936]

Table A10. Equation 4: log[Rail (goods)] - Heteroskedasticity-robust standard errors

	Coefficient	Std. Error	t-ratio	p-value	
const	6.35863	20.2592	0.3139	0.75723	
log[Air (goods)]	-0.224531	0.116046	-1.9349	0.06888	*
log[Air (passengers)]	0.150125	0.103867	1.4454	0.16554	
log[Rail total]	-0.0523306	2.14712	-0.0244	0.98082	
log[Rail (goods)]	0.133035	0.18399	0.7231	0.47894	
log[Rail (passengers)]	0.126508	0.257606	0.4911	0.62930	
log[Diesel consumption (per capita)]	1.17189	0.432731	2.7081	0.01440	**
log[Road energy consumption (per capita)]	-1.84126	0.879117	-2.0944	0.05064	*
log[Gasoline consumption (per capita)]	0.790966	0.298663	2.6484	0.01635	**
log[GDP (per capita)]	-0.0326127	0.097366	-0.3349	0.74154	
time	0.0457923	0.0198132	2.3112	0.03287	**

Table A11. Descriptive statistics of Equation 4

Mean dependent var	9.004348	S.D. dependent var	0.144406
Sum squared resid	0.093620	S.E. of regression	0.072119
R-squared	0.839661	Adjusted R-squared	0.750583
F(10, 18)	16.24854	P-value(F)	4.79e-07
rho	-0.011175	Durbin-Watson	1.969770

Table A12. F-tests of zero restrictions of Equation 4

All lags of log[Air (goods)]	$F(1, 18) = 3.7436 \, [0.0689]$
All lags of log[Air (passengers)]	$F(1, 18) = 2.0891 \, [0.1655]$
All lags of log[Rail total]	$F(1, 18) = 0.00059402 \, [0.9808]$
All lags of log[Rail (goods)]	$F(1, 18) = 0.52281 \, [0.4789]$
All lags of log[Rail (passengers)]	$F(1, 18) = 0.24117 \, [0.6293]$
All lags of log[Diesel consumption (per capita)]	$F(1, 18) = 7.334 \, [0.0144]$
All lags of log[Road energy consumption (per capita)]	$F(1, 18) = 4.3867 \, [0.0506]$
All lags of log[Gasoline consumption (per capita)]	$F(1, 18) = 7.0138 \, [0.0163]$
All lags of log[GDP (per capita)]	$F(1, 18) = 0.11219 \, [0.7415]$

Table A13. Equation 5: log[Rail (passengers)] - Heteroskedasticity-robust standard errors

	Coefficient	Std. Error	t-ratio	p-value	
const	52.7654	26.054	2.0252	0.05793	*
log[Air (goods)]	-0.0519624	0.0705297	-0.7367	0.47077	
log[Air (passengers)]	-0.152938	0.124728	-1.2262	0.23593	
log[Rail total]	-5.04656	2.67983	-1.8832	0.07594	*
log[Rail (goods)]	0.115067	0.163513	0.7037	0.49061	
log[Rail (passengers)]	0.232056	0.203043	1.1429	0.26806	
log[Diesel consumption (per capita)]	0.0525678	0.362947	0.1448	0.88645	
log[Road energy consumption (per capita)]	-0.178645	0.707355	-0.2526	0.80347	
log[Gasoline consumption (per capita)]	0.28541	0.225375	1.2664	0.22152	
log[GDP (per capita)]	0.025678	0.091775	0.2798	0.78283	
time	0.0301208	0.0143253	2.1026	0.04983	**

Table A14. Descriptive statistics of Equation 5

Mean dependent var	8.678902	S.D. dependent var	0.092983
Sum squared resid	0.078527	S.E. of regression	0.066050
R-squared	0.675617	Adjusted R-squared	0.495404
$F(10, 18)$	11.25203	P-value(F)	7.60e-06
rho	-0.066043	Durbin-Watson	2.114679

Table A15. F-tests of zero restrictions of Equation 5

All lags of log[Air (goods)]	$F(1, 18) = 0.54279$ [0.4708]
All lags of log[Air (passengers)]	$F(1, 18) = 1.5035$ [0.2359]
All lags of log[Rail total]	$F(1, 18) = 3.5463$ [0.0759]
All lags of log[Rail (goods)]	$F(1, 18) = 0.49522$ [0.4906]
All lags of log[Rail (passengers)]	$F(1, 18) = 1.3062$ [0.2681]
All lags of log[Diesel consumption (per capita)]	$F(1, 18) = 0.020977$ [0.8864]
All lags of log[Road energy consumption (per capita)]	$F(1, 18) = 0.063784$ [0.8035]
All lags of log[Gasoline consumption (per capita)]	$F(1, 18) = 1.6037$ [0.2215]
All lags of log[GDP (per capita)]	$F(1, 18) = 0.078284$ [0.7828]

Table A16. Equation 6: log[Diesel consumption (per capita)] - Heteroskedasticity-robust standard errors

	Coefficient	Std. Error	t-ratio	p-value	
const	66.3927	27.3234	2.4299	0.02579	**
log[Air (goods)]	0.178299	0.115278	1.5467	0.13934	
log[Air (passengers)]	0.106854	0.146597	0.7289	0.47544	
log[Rail total]	-7.13494	2.91481	-2.4478	0.02485	**
log[Rail (goods)]	-0.391253	0.287906	-1.3590	0.19094	
log[Rail (passengers)]	0.448956	0.314776	1.4263	0.17090	
log[Diesel consumption (per capita)]	1.38521	0.51435	2.6931	0.01487	**
log[Road energy consumption (per capita)]	-1.84225	0.949724	-1.9398	0.06824	*
log[Gasoline consumption (per capita)]	0.301422	0.286609	1.0517	0.30686	
log[GDP (per capita)]	0.173921	0.12516	1.3896	0.18160	
time	0.0106616	0.0172679	0.6174	0.54469	

Table A17. Descriptive statistics of Equation 6

Mean dependent var	4.465014	S.D. dependent var	0.197953
Sum squared resid	0.159557	S.E. of regression	0.094150
R-squared	0.854577	Adjusted R-squared	0.773786
F(10, 18)	20.68094	P-value(F)	7.17e-08
rho	-0.098488	Durbin-Watson	2.168914

Table A18. F-tests of zero restrictions of Equation 6

All lags of log[Air (goods)]	$F(1, 18) =$ 2.3922 [0.1393]
All lags of log[Air (passengers)]	$F(1, 18) =$ 0.53129 [0.4754]
All lags of log[Rail total]	$F(1, 18) =$ 5.9919 [0.0249]
All lags of log[Rail (goods)]	$F(1, 18) =$ 1.8468 [0.1909]
All lags of log[Rail (passengers)]	$F(1, 18) =$ 2.0342 [0.1709]
All lags of log[Diesel consumption (per capita)]	$F(1, 18) =$ 7.2529 [0.0149]
All lags of log[Road energy consumption (per capita)]	$F(1, 18) =$ 3.7627 [0.0682]
All lags of log[Gasoline consumption (per capita)]	$F(1, 18) =$ 1.106 [0.3069]
All lags of log[GDP (per capita)]	$F(1, 18) =$ 1.931 [0.1816]

Table A19. Equation 7: log[Road energy consumption (per capita)] - Heteroskedasticity-robust standard errors

	Coefficient	Std. Error	t-ratio	p-value	
const	33.2058	23.4738	1.4146	0.17426	
log[Air (goods)]	0.0713808	0.0958049	0.7451	0.46585	
log[Air (passengers)]	0.108126	0.101965	1.0604	0.30297	
log[Rail total]	-3.51632	2.47206	-1.4224	0.17200	
log[Rail (goods)]	-0.124773	0.160125	-0.7792	0.44597	
log[Rail (passengers)]	0.200977	0.240042	0.8373	0.41343	
log[Diesel consumption (per capita)]	0.826922	0.329752	2.5077	0.02195	**
log[Road energy consumption (per capita)]	-1.14068	0.619717	-1.8406	0.08222	*
log[Gasoline consumption (per capita)]	0.489366	0.211226	2.3168	0.03250	**
log[GDP (per capita)]	0.112687	0.0892835	1.2621	0.22301	
time	0.0106075	0.0147734	0.7180	0.48196	

Table A20. Descriptive statistics of Equation 7

Mean dependent var	5.017339	S.D. dependent var	0.167491
Sum squared resid	0.071550	S.E. of regression	0.063048
R-squared	0.908910	Adjusted R-squared	0.858304
F(10, 18)	40.33409	P-value(F)	2.90e-10
rho	-0.128539	Durbin-Watson	2.236902

Table A21. F-tests of zero restrictions of Equation 7

All lags of log[Air (goods)]	$F(1, 18) =$ 0.55512 [0.4659]
All lags of log[Air (passengers)]	$F(1, 18) =$ 1.1245 [0.3030]
All lags of log[Rail total]	$F(1, 18) =$ 2.0233 [0.1720]
All lags of log[Rail (goods)]	$F(1, 18) =$ 0.60719 [0.4460]
All lags of log[Rail (passengers)]	$F(1, 18) =$ 0.701 [0.4134]
All lags of log[Diesel consumption (per capita)]	$F(1, 18) =$ 6.2886 [0.0220]
All lags of log[Road energy consumption (per capita)]	$F(1, 18) =$ 3.388 [0.0822]
All lags of log[Gasoline consumption (per capita)]	$F(1, 18) =$ 5.3675 [0.0325]
All lags of log[GDP (per capita)]	$F(1, 18) =$ 1.593 [0.2230]

Table A22. Equation 8: log[Gasoline consumption (per capita)] - Heteroskedasticity-robust standard errors

	Coefficient	Std. Error	t-ratio	p-value	
const	3.61602	30.7798	0.1175	0.90778	
log[Air (goods)]	0.0549476	0.17572	0.3127	0.75810	
log[Air (passengers)]	0.0312166	0.17401	0.1794	0.85963	
log[Rail total]	-0.378358	3.20278	-0.1181	0.90727	
log[Rail (goods)]	0.139164	0.278158	0.5003	0.62292	
log[Rail (passengers)]	-0.021565	0.296843	-0.0726	0.94289	
log[Diesel consumption (per capita)]	0.986728	0.621087	1.5887	0.12954	
log[Road energy consumption (per capita)]	-1.692	1.17312	-1.4423	0.16639	
log[Gasoline consumption (per capita)]	1.38376	0.415444	3.3308	0.00372	***
log[GDP (per capita)]	0.0814216	0.161454	0.5043	0.62017	
time	-0.00575877	0.0289877	-0.1987	0.84475	

Table A23. Descriptive statistics of Equation 8

Mean dependent var	3.897209	S.D. dependent var	0.268196
Sum squared resid	0.151016	S.E. of regression	0.091596
R-squared	0.925017	Adjusted R-squared	0.883361
F(10, 18)	68.09901	P-value(F)	3.24e-12
rho	-0.249614	Durbin-Watson	2.477735

Table A24. F-tests of zero restrictions of Equation 8

All lags of log[Air (goods)]	$F(1, 18) = 0.097782\ [0.7581]$
All lags of log[Air (passengers)]	$F(1, 18) = 0.032183\ [0.8596]$
All lags of log[Rail total]	$F(1, 18) = 0.013956\ [0.9073]$
All lags of log[Rail (goods)]	$F(1, 18) = 0.25031\ [0.6229]$
All lags of log[Rail (passengers)]	$F(1, 18) = 0.0052777\ [0.9429]$
All lags of log[Diesel consumption (per capita)]	$F(1, 18) = 2.524\ [0.1295]$
All lags of log[Road energy consumption (per capita)]	$F(1, 18) = 2.0802\ [0.1664]$
All lags of log[Gasoline consumption (per capita)]	$F(1, 18) = 11.094\ [0.0037]$
All lags of log[GDP (per capita)]	$F(1, 18) = 0.25432\ [0.6202]$

Table A25. Equation 9: log[GDP (per capita)] - Heteroskedasticity-robust standard errors

	Coefficient	Std. Error	t-ratio	p-value	
const	-47.4606	55.0484	-0.8622	0.39994	
log[Air (goods)]	-0.339759	0.292634	-1.1610	0.26079	
log[Air (passengers)]	-0.00325667	0.283511	-0.0115	0.99096	
log[Rail total]	5.66311	5.8301	0.9714	0.34424	
log[Rail (goods)]	0.0115694	0.586428	0.0197	0.98448	
log[Rail (passengers)]	0.362407	0.6771	0.5352	0.59904	
log[Diesel consumption (per capita)]	1.26123	1.35061	0.9338	0.36276	
log[Road energy consumption (per capita)]	-2.07875	2.47366	-0.8404	0.41173	
log[Gasoline consumption (per capita)]	0.647419	0.894305	0.7239	0.47841	
log[GDP (per capita)]	0.446238	0.203776	2.1899	0.04195	**
time	0.0891398	0.0493434	1.8065	0.08758	*

Table A26. Descriptive statistics of Equation 9

Mean dependent var	8.037601	S.D. dependent var	0.624577
Sum squared resid	0.441576	S.E. of regression	0.156627
R-squared	0.959573	Adjusted R-squared	0.937113
F(10, 18)	168.4143	P-value(F)	1.14e-15
rho	-0.127236	Durbin-Watson	2.171390

Table A27. F-tests of zero restrictions of Equation 9

All lags of log[Air (goods)]	$F(1, 18) = $ 1.348 [0.2608]
All lags of log[Air (passengers)]	$F(1, 18) = $ 0.00013195 [0.9910]
All lags of log[Rail total]	$F(1, 18) = $ 0.94353 [0.3442]
All lags of log[Rail (goods)]	$F(1, 18) = $ 0.00038922 [0.9845]
All lags of log[Rail (passengers)]	$F(1, 18) = $ 0.28647 [0.5990]
All lags of log[Diesel consumption (per capita)]	$F(1, 18) = $ 0.87202 [0.3628]
All lags of log[Road energy consumption (per capita)]	$F(1, 18) = $ 0.7062 [0.4117]
All lags of log[Gasoline consumption (per capita)]	$F(1, 18) = $ 0.52408 [0.4784]
All lags of log[GDP (per capita)]	$F(1, 18) = $ 4.7954 [0.0419]

ABOUT THE AUTHOR

Turkay Yildiz received his Ph.D. from the Institute of Marine Sciences and Technology, Dokuz Eylul University, Izmir, Turkey. He received his Master's Degree in Logistics Management from Izmir University of Economics. He has a number of peer reviewed publications and conference presentations at various countries in such fields as transportation, logistics and supply chains. He also has various levels of expertise in the applications of Information Technology.

www.ingramcontent.com/pod-product-compliance
Lightning Source LLC
Chambersburg PA
CBHW070616300426
44113CB00010B/1550